Confucius from the Heart

Yu Dan

Confucius
from the Heart

Ancient Wisdom for Today's World

Translated by Esther Tyldesley

MACMILLAN

Contents

Foreword – Why Confucius?

Over two thousand five hundred years ago, the students of the thinker and philosopher Confucius wrote down every scrap and scattered fragment of his life and teachings that they could find. These records, based for the most part on classroom notes, were compiled and edited, and afterwards they became what we know as *The Analects of Confucius*. 'Analects' simply means a collection of writings.

Just over two thousand years ago, the great Han Dynasty emperor Wu rejected a hundred other philosophical schools in favour of Confucius, effectively making China a Confucian state.

A thousand years ago the first prime minister of the Song Dynasty, Zhao Pu, boasted that he could rule the known world with just half a book of the *Analects*. From this we can see the tremendously important role that Confucius played in the political and social life of ancient times, and the high esteem in which his collected teachings were held by the ancients.

But what practical meaning do they have for our society and our lives today?

When I entrusted the manuscript of my book to the Zhonghua Book Company in China at the end of 2006, I was content but also a little troubled. I started my master's degree in pre-Qin Dynasty literature at the age of twenty-one, and I had grown up immersed in books from the Zhonghua Book Company, but I would never have dared to dream that one day this elite publishing house might bring out a book of mine, no more than I would have presumed to entertain the hope that I would ever dare to stand up and talk about *The Analects of Confucius* on television

I have always respected this book rather than fearing it, and my feelings towards it have always been plain, simple and warm.

Once, in a small town in north China, famous for its hot springs, I saw something called the 'Ask Sickness Spring'. It is said that anybody who takes a comfortable soak in its water will at once understand the source of their illness: people with arthritis will get a tingling feeling in their joints, those with gastro-intestinal problems will experience a hot sensation in their gut, while people with skin complaints will feel a pleasant flush all over their skin, as if a layer of skin is being washed away, like the sloughed-off skin of a cicada.

For me, the wisdom of Confucius is just such a spring of warm, living water.

With my limited knowledge, even if I truly wanted to write an in-depth analysis of Confucius, I would never, ever dare to do such a thing. It would be like sending me off to make a chemical analysis of that hot spring, when I am totally unequipped to do so. The only possible role for me is that of someone who has been immersed in the spring myself, testing it with my own body and blood, like the thousands and thousands of people who over the last two hundred years and more have steeped themselves in this hot spring, and experienced its gifts.

The good will see goodness in it, and the wise see wisdom. Perhaps the value of this classical text is not in rituals and reverence that inspire awe and fear, but in its inclusiveness and fluidity, the wisdom in which so many people have immersed themselves down the ages, so that every life and every individual, though perceiving it differently, and following different paths, can arrive at last at the same final goal. In China we say 'The truth has never been far away from ordinary people' and here that is certainly the case.

It seems to me that the sages never used obscure classical quotations to intimidate people, nor did they load their writing with fancy phrases and difficult words to shut them out. Confucius said: 'I am thinking of giving up speech.' Zigong said hastily: 'If you did not speak, what would there be for us, your disciples, to transmit?' Confucius said, calmly and matter-of-factly: 'What does Heaven ever say? Yet there are the four seasons going round and there are the hundred things coming into being. What does Heaven ever say?'

The easy truths of this world can enter into people's hearts because they have never been about indoctrination, but rather an inner call to wake up every heart and soul.

The reason why these simple truths have survived down the millennia is that they have helped generation after generation of Chinese to stay grounded, to understand the nation and the culture that formed them, and not to lose their heads, even when confronted by immense social change and almost overwhelming choice.

Those who benefit from the wisdom of Confucius may experience a moment's heart-stopping enlightenment, in which understanding suddenly floods through them; equally, they may undertake a lifetime of endless study in order to attain understanding.

I really must thank the television programme *Lecture Room* for encouraging me to approach Confucius from this angle of *'xinde'* – an understanding that comes from the heart as much as the head. A thousand hearts will get a thousand different things out of his work, ten thousand will get ten thousand different things from it, and mine is no more than the understanding of one heart among many. When we read it in the course of our lives today, and everything suddenly becomes clear to us, Confucius must surely be smiling silently on us from across the centuries.

The Song Dynasty prime minister Zhao Pu's boast is a respectful acknowledgement of Confucius as the source of Chinese traditional culture and thought. I, however, would rather say: 'With half a book of the *Analects* I can enrich myself.' Everybody should see it as a warm, gentle 'Ask Sickness Spring'.

Therefore what we can learn from Confucius today is not the 'Confucian Learning' set out by Emperor Wu; it is not the solemn, dignified, ritualized 'Confucian religion' that stands alongside Daoism and Buddhism in China; nor is it the Confucianism of the scholars, full of deep argumentation and fettered by textual research.

What we can take away from the *Analects* of Confucius are the simple truths that every person knows in his or her heart, though they may not let them out through their mouths.

In my view, the wisdom of Confucius does not burn your hands, nor is it icy cold, its temperature is just slightly above body heat, for it is a constant that will remain the same throughout the ages.

Midnight, 16 November 2006

Part One

The Way of
Heaven and Earth

You should not think that the wisdom of Confucius is lofty and out of reach, or something that people today can only look up to with reverence.

The truths of this world are for ever plain and simple, in the same way that the sun rises every day in the east, just as spring is the time for sowing and autumn is the time to harvest.

The truths that Confucius gives us are always the easiest of truths.

They tell us all how we can live the kind of happy life that our spirit needs.

The wisdom of Confucius can help us to obtain spiritual happiness in the modern world, to get used to the daily routine of our lives, and to find the personal bearings that tell us where we are.

We might sometimes think that what we read lacks a rigorous logic. Very many of the sayings concentrate on a single issue, there are few passages of any great length, and almost everything we find is simple and short.

We will see how this absence of words is also a kind of teaching.

Confucius said: 'What does Heaven ever say? Yet there are the four seasons going round and there are the hundred things coming into being. What does Heaven ever say?' (*Analects* xvii) Confucius said: See, the heavens are above us, solemn and quiet, never speaking a word, yet the four seasons come round again and again, and all of nature increases and multiplies around us. Do the heavens need to speak as well?

What we will find in Confucius is a way of thinking, which is plain, simple and warm. It is exactly this attitude with which Confucius influenced his students.

Confucius had three thousand students, seventy-two of whom were men of exceptional wisdom and virtue. Each of these men was a seed, and each in his turn spread the seed of this wisdom and this view of life far and wide.

That is why in China we call Confucius a sage. The sages are those people who in their time on this earth are the most practical and capable, and possess the most personal magnetism. They bring us conviction, and a kind of faith. Such men can only be the product of natural growth, emerging from within our lives, not dropping down from heaven.

This sense of natural, balanced growth can be found in China's creation myth, which tells of Pan Gu, who separated heaven and earth. This separation was not a sudden change, as in a Western creation myth, where Pan Gu might be expected to take a big axe and split them apart with a bang, whereupon a golden light might perhaps shine out in all directions, and the heavens, earth and everything in them all appear at once. That is not the Chinese style.

The type of story that Chinese people are used to is like that described in the *San Wu Li Ji*, our very early

Chinese history, which includes stories of how the world was made. Here we find that creation was a very lengthy process: calm, relaxed and full of anticipation:

Heaven and earth were jumbled together in a cosmic egg for eighteen thousand years, and Pan Gu lived in the midst of it. The heavens and the earth split apart. The pure Yang essence became the heavens, the heavy Yin essence was the earth. Pan Gu was between them, nine changes in one day, a god in the heavens and a sage on the earth. Every day the heavens rose higher by ten feet, the earth grew thicker by ten feet, and Pan Gu became ten feet taller. When he reached eighteen thousand years of age, the heavens were infinitely high, the earth was infinitely deep, and Pan Gu was infinitely tall.

Afterwards, heaven and earth split apart, not in the way that a solid body splits in two with a crack, but rather as a gradual separation of two essences; the light, pure *yang* essence rose up and became the heavens, the heavy *yin* essence sank and became the earth.

But that was not the end of the separation of heaven and earth. The process had only just begun.

Notice how Chinese people pay a lot of attention to

changes. Look at Pan Gu, who in between the heavens and the earth went through 'nine changes in one day': just like a newborn baby, tiny, subtle changes were taking place every day.

There is a stage in the changes which the text calls 'a god in the heavens, a sage on earth' when Pan Gu had become a wise and powerful being in both realms.

For the Chinese, this idea of mastery in both realms is an ideal way of being, one to which we should all aspire: a heaven where idealism can spread its wings and fly freely, with no need to compromise with all the rules and obstacles of the real world; and the ability to keep our feet planted firmly on the ground, so that we can make our way in the real world.

People who have only ambition and no realism are dreamers, not idealists; those who have only earth and no sky are plodders, not realists.

Idealism and realism are our heaven and earth.

But Pan Gu's changes are still going on and our story continues.

After the heavens and the earth had separated, every day the heavens became higher by ten feet, the earth gained ten feet in thickness, and Pan Gu 'grew ten feet every day', along with the heavens.

In this way another eighteen thousand years passed,

until at last 'the heavens were infinitely high, the earth was infinitely deep, and Pan Gu was infinitely tall'.

In other words, humankind is equal to the heavens and the earth: heaven, earth and people are referred to together as the Three Realms – the three equally great and important things from which the world is made.

Confucius viewed the world in this way: human beings are worthy of respect, and people should respect themselves.

When reading *The Analects of Confucius* we find that Confucius very seldom spoke harshly or sternly to his students, he usually talked things over with them in a relaxed, easy manner, giving them clues and hints so that they could work things out for themselves. We have all seen teachers scold their students, telling them not to do this or that. That is what happens when a teacher is not all he or she should be. A truly excellent teacher will be like Confucius, peacefully exchanging views with their students, together getting to the heart of how to make these Three Realms of heaven, earth and humanity all prosper and flourish together.

This relaxed, unhurried, assured spirit and modest, respectful attitude is something we should all aspire to. *The Analects of Confucius* is the embodiment of this ideal.

> Our ultimate aim is to let the key principles of Confucius
> enter into our hearts, uniting Heaven, Earth and
> humankind in a perfect whole, and giving us
> infinite strength.
>
> In China today we often say that for a nation to
> survive and prosper, Heaven must smile on it, the Earth
> must be favourable to it and its people must be at peace.
> It is to this harmonious balance that Confucius
> can lead us today.

From it we can derive great strength, a strength that flowed from Confucius's inner heart. It is this strength that Mencius, another of China's great philosophers, who came after Confucius and further developed his ideas, described as 'the noble spirit'.

Only when the essences of Heaven, Earth and everything in between them combine within a person's heart, can they be as powerful as this.

What do we mean by heaven and humanity becoming one? We mean humankind and the natural world in perfect harmony.

We are working hard to create a harmonious society,

but what is true harmony? It is more than just harmony within a small housing estate, nor is it merely cordial relations between people. It must also include the entire natural world, harmoniously and happily living and growing together on this earth. People should feel reverence for the natural world and a willingness to follow its rhythms.

This is a kind of strength. If we learn how to temper this strength, and to draw on it, then we will be able to attain a breadth of mind like that of Confucius.

Confucius's attitude was extremely placid, yet his inner heart was very serious. This was because he had a deep strength within him, rooted in the strength of his convictions.

His student Zigong once asked him what conditions were necessary for a country to be at peace, with a stable government. Confucius's reply was very simple. There were only three: enough arms, enough food and the trust of the common people.

First, the internal apparatus of the state must be powerful, it must have enough military power to protect itself.

Second, it must have sufficient supplies, so its people can be well fed and clothed.

Third, the common people must have belief in the nation.

This student was always full of awkward questions. He said that three conditions were too many: Tell me, if you have to do without one of these, which one would you remove first?

Confucius said: 'Give up arms.' So we'll do without military protection.

Zigong asked again: If you had to get rid of another one, which would you give up?

Confucius in all seriousness told him: 'Give up food.' We are willing not to eat.

He continued: 'Death has always been with us since the beginning of time, but when there is no trust, the common people will have nothing to stand on.'

To do without food will certainly lead to death, but from ancient times to this day has anyone ever cheated death? So death is not the worst thing that can happen. The most terrible thing of all is the collapse and breakdown that follow when a country's citizens give up on their nation.

On a material level, a happy life is no more than a series of goals to be reached; but true peace and stability come from within, from an acceptance of those that govern us, and this comes from faith.

This is Confucius's concept of government. He

believed that the power of faith alone was sufficient to hold a nation together.

In the twenty-first century we say that it is no longer enough to use the simplistic standard of GNP (Gross National Product) to assess the quality of the people's life in different countries. You must also look at GNH: Gross National Happiness.

In other words, to evaluate whether a country is truly rich and powerful, you should not just look at the speed and scale of its economic growth, you should look more at the feelings in the heart of each ordinary citizen – Do I feel safe? Am I happy? Do I truly identify with the life I lead?

At the end of the 1980s, China took part in an international survey, which showed that at that time the happiness of our citizens was only around 64 per cent.

In 1991 we took part in the survey again. The happiness index had risen, reaching around 73 per cent. This came from an improvement in our standard of living, as well as all the reforms that were being carried out around then.

But by the time we took part for a third time, in 1996, the happiness index had fallen to 68 per cent.

This is a very puzzling business. It shows that even

when a society is thriving materially and culturally, the people who enjoy the fruits of that society may nonetheless experience an extremely complex kind of spiritual bewilderment.

Let us travel back in time two thousand five hundred years, and compare what the sages and wise men were like in this less prosperous age.

Confucius was very fond of a student called Yan Hui. On one occasion he praised him: 'How admirable Hui is! Living in a mean dwelling on a bowlful of rice and a ladleful of water is a hardship most men would find intolerable, but Hui does not allow this to affect his joy. How admirable Hui is!' (*Analects* VI)

Yan Hui's family was very poor. They never had enough to eat or new clothes to wear, and lived in a grim, run-down little alley. For most people, a hard life like this would be simply unendurable, yet Yan Hui could find happiness in what he had.

Perhaps many people would say: 'That's just the way life is, we all have to live, rich or poor, what can be done about it?'

What is truly admirable about Yan Hui is not that he could endure such rough living conditions, but his attitude to life. When everybody was sighing bitterly and complaining about how hard life is, Yan Hui's optimism never wavered.

We see that only the truly enlightened can avoid becoming tied down by the material things in life and keep a calm, tranquil mindset from start to finish, indifferent to fame or personal gain.

Of course, nobody wants to live a hard life, but equally, we cannot solve our spiritual problems through a dependence on more and more possessions.

In modern China, our lives are visibly improving in a material sense, yet a great many people are growing more and more dissatisfied. Because we have a highly visible class of people who have suddenly become extremely wealthy, there is always something to make ordinary people feel that their lives contain unfairness.

Actually, what we focus on can work in two ways: one is outward-looking, infinitely broad, expanding our world; another is inward-looking, delving infinitely deep to explore the inner heart.

We always spend too much time looking at the outside world, and too little looking at our hearts and souls.

Confucius can teach us the secret of happiness, which is how to find the peace within us.

A student, Zigong, once asked Confucius: ' "Poor

Everybody hopes to live a happy life, but happiness is only a feeling, which has nothing to do with wealth or poverty, but with the inner heart.

Confucius tells his students how to look for happiness in life. This philosophy has been passed down over the ages, and had a profound influence on a great many of our famous scholars and poets.

without being obsequious, wealthy without being arrogant." What do you think of this saying?' Imagine somebody who is very poor but doesn't grovel to the rich, or someone who is very rich and powerful but not haughty or arrogant. What do you think of that?

Confucius told him this is pretty good, but it is still not enough. There is another, higher state: 'Poor yet delighting in the Way, wealthy yet observant of the rites.'

The higher state requires that a person must not only accept poverty peaceably, and not go crawling and begging for favours, but they must also be possessed of a calm, clear inner happiness, the kind of happiness that cannot be taken away by a life of poverty. Neither will power and riches make such a person haughty or self-indulgent: they will still be refined and courteous, with a cheerful, contented mind. Such a person can both avoid being led astray by a life of wealth and plenty, and can keep their self-respect and inner happiness. Such a person can truly be called a *junzi*.

The word *junzi*, which appears more often than any other in *The Analects of Confucius*, describes Confucius's ideal person, who any one of us, rich or poor, has the potential to become. To this day, in China, we still use the word as a standard for personal integrity, saying that such and such a person is a real *junzi*. As Confucius's ideas were passed down the generations, they shaped the many great-hearted *junzi* who appear throughout our history and whom we can learn from as we strive to become *junzi* in our own lives.

Tao Yuanming, the great poet of the Eastern Jin Dynasty, was one such figure. For eighty-three days he held a minor official post of Magistrate of Pengze, until one very small thing led him to reject his post and return home.

He was told that his superiors were sending someone to inspect his work and that he should 'tie your robes with a belt to greet him', just as today you would wear a suit and tie to show respect to visiting leaders.

Tao Yuanming said: 'I can't bow low like a servant for the sake of five measures of rice.' In other words he was not prepared to grovel for the sake of an official's tiny salary. And so he went back home, leaving his seal of office behind.

> Our eyes see too much of the word, and too little of the heart and soul.

When he got there, he wrote down what he felt.

He said: 'Since my heart has become the slave of my body, I feel melancholy and grieved.' He felt that just in

---

In modern people's eyes, to be content to be poor while holding fast to one's principles tends to imply a certain lack of get up and go. Everybody is working hard to develop their own career in the face of fierce competition, and it seems that how much a person earns, and their professional status (or lack of it), has become the most important sign of success.

But the fiercer the competition, the more we need to adjust our outlook, and our relationships with others. With this in mind, how should we conduct ourselves in modern society? Are there rules to guide us?

order to eat a little better and have somewhere slightly better to live, he had no choice but to abase himself, grovel and curry favour.

He was not willing to live such a life – 'I know that I cannot return to my past, but I know my own future and can pursue it' – and so he returned once more to his beloved countryside.

Zigong again asked Confucius an extremely important question: 'Is there a single word which can be a guide to conduct throughout one's life?' Can you give me one word that I will be able use until the end of my days, and always derive benefit from it?

Confucius replied to him in a conversational tone of voice: 'If such a word exists, it is probably the word *shu*, or "forbearance".'

But what do we mean by this? Confucius went on: 'Do not impose on others what you yourself do not desire.' That is, you mustn't force other people to do the things you don't want to do yourself. If a person can do this throughout their life, that is enough.

And this is what is meant by 'With half a book of *The Analects of Confucius* I can govern the Empire.' Sometimes learning one word or a couple of words is enough to last us a whole lifetime.

Confucius is a true sage – he won't give you so very

much to remember, and sometimes a single word is all you need.

Confucius's disciple Zengzi once said: 'The way of the Master consists in doing one's best and in using oneself as a measure to gauge others. That is all.' The essence of Confucius's teaching can be distilled into just the two words 'faithfulness' and 'forbearance'. Put simply, you have to be yourself, but at the same time you must think about others.

By forbearance, Confucius means that you mustn't force people to do things against their will, nor must you do things to hurt others. By extension, he means that if other people do things that hurt you, you must do the best you can to treat them with tolerance.

But this is often easier said than done. Often, when something unfair or unjust happens, we can't help brooding, going over it constantly. And by doing so, we are hurt over and over again.

There is an interesting tale in Buddhism.

Two monks came down from their mountain temple to beg alms. When they reached the bank of a river, they saw a girl, who was upset because she was unable to cross it. The old monk said to the girl: 'I'll carry you over on my back.' And he gave the girl a piggy-back across the river.

The young monk was too shocked to do anything

more than gape in astonishment. He didn't dare to ask any questions. They walked on for another twenty leagues, and at last he could bear it no longer, so he asked the old monk: 'Master, we're monks, we're supposed to be celibate, how could you carry a girl across the river on your back?'

Being tolerant of others is actually leaving yourself a lot more room.

The old monk said coolly: 'You saw how I got her across the river and then put her down. How come you have carried this thought with you for twenty leagues and yet you still haven't put it down?'

The moral of this story is exactly what Confucius teaches us: when it's time to put things down, put them down. By being tolerant of others, you are in fact leaving yourself a lot more room.

But what Confucius tells us is not just that we should let ourselves pick things up or let them drop, but that we also should do everything we can to give help to those who need it. This is what we mean by 'If you give a rose, the scent will remain on your hands': giving can bring more happiness than receiving.

There is a third word, besides faithfulness and forbearance, at the very centre of Confucian theory: 'benevolence'.

Confucius's student Fan Chi once respectfully asked his teacher: 'What is benevolence?' The teacher answered in two words: 'Loving people.' Loving other people is benevolence.

Fan Chi asked again: 'What is this thing called wisdom?' The teacher said: 'Knowing people.' The understanding of others is called wisdom.

To love and care for others is benevolence; to understand others is wisdom. It's as simple as that.

So what is the best way to be a person with a benevolent, loving heart?

Confucius said: 'A benevolent man helps others to take their stand in so far as he himself wishes to take his stand, and gets others there in so far as he himself wishes to get there. The ability to take as analogy what is near at hand can be called the method of benevolence.' (*Analects* VI)

If you wish to raise yourself up, immediately think of how to help other people raise themselves up too; if you want to realize your own ambition, think at once of how to help other people to realize their ambitions. This can be done starting with the small things near to you, treating others as you would like to be treated yourself. This is the way to live according to benevolence and justice.

In life, any one of us may experience sudden unemployment, marriage breakdown, betrayal by a friend, or abandonment by someone close to us, and we may regard it as either something serious or something minor; there is no objective standard.

For example, if you get a cut, perhaps an inch long, does this count as a severe injury, or a minor one? A delicate, sensitive young girl might make a fuss about something like this for a whole week; but a big, tough young man might simply not notice, from when the cut was made to when it healed by itself.

So, whether we take on the role of a delicate 'young girl' or a strong 'young man' is something that is entirely up to us.

If you have an infinitely broad mind, you will always be able to keep things in their proper perspective.

I remember a story from my university English coursebook, about a king who spent every day pondering three ultimate questions: Who is the most important person in this world? What is the most important thing? When is the most important time to do things?

He put these three questions to his court and his ministers, but nobody could give him an answer and he was very downhearted.

Afterwards, one day he went out dressed as a commoner and walked to a remote place, where he took shelter for the night in an old man's house.

In the middle of the night, he woke with a start to hear a racket outside, and he saw that a man covered in blood had rushed into the old man's home.

That man said: 'There are men after me, they're going to arrest me!' The old man said: 'Then take shelter with me here for a while' and hid him away.

The king was too frightened to sleep, and soon he saw soldiers come running up, hot on the trail. The soldiers asked the old man if he had seen anyone come past. The old man said: 'I don't know, there's nobody else here.'

To love and care for other people is benevolence; to understand other people is righteousness.

Afterwards the soldiers went away. The man they had been chasing said a few words of gratitude and left. The old man shut the door and went back to sleep.

The next day the king said to the old man: 'Why weren't you afraid to take in that man? Weren't you afraid of causing terrible trouble? It might have cost you your life! And then you just let him go like that. Why didn't you ask who he was?'

The old man said calmly: 'In this world, the most important person is the person in front of you who needs your help, the most important thing is to help them, and the most important time is right now, you can't delay, not even for an instant.'

It all suddenly became clear to the king: those three philosophical questions he had been pondering for so long were solved in that instant.

This story can also be used as a footnote to reading Confucius.

What is most significant about people like Confucius or any of the other great thinkers from China and abroad, past and present, is that they drew from their own practical experiences of life, truths and principles that everybody can use.

These truths are not found in the pages of massive volumes of the classics and ancient records, the kind you need a magnifying glass and an enormous dictionary to read and that will take you a lifetime's laborious study to understand.

The true sages wouldn't put on airs or speak with a stern, forbidding face. They have passed down to us their living, breathing experience of human life, through all the great, sweeping changes the world has gone through, so that we can still feel its warmth. From a thousand years ago, they are smiling on down us, watching us in silence as we continue to reap the benefits of their words.

Confucius offers us simple truths that will help us develop our inner hearts and souls and allow us to make the right choices as we go through life's journey. The first step on this journey is having the right attitude.

Part Two

The Way of
the Heart and Soul

As we move through life, it is hard for us to avoid things that cause regret and disappointment. We may lack the strength to change this, but what we can change is the attitude with which we approach these setbacks.

One of the most important things about Confucius is that he tells us how to face regret and suffering with a tranquil mind.

But can wisdom from two and a half thousand years ago, truly unravel the knots and tangles in the hearts of people today?

We are on this planet for a whole lifetime, how can our lives be free from regret? In this life, people will always find something or other that does not go as they would wish.

Confucius had three thousand students, of whom seventy-two were men of unusual wisdom and virtue, and every single one of these students had things that grieved him. So how did they view the regrets of human life?

One day, Confucius's student Sima Niu, said sorrowfully: 'Everybody else has brothers, why am I the only one without?'

His classmate Zixia consoled him, saying: 'I have heard it said: life and death are a matter of Destiny; wealth and honour depend on Heaven. The *junzi* is reverent and does nothing amiss, is respectful towards others and observant of the rites, and all within the Four Seas are his brothers. What need is there for the *junzi* to worry about not having any brothers?'

These words can be read on several different levels.

Since life and death, wealth and prestige and all such things are determined by fate, they are beyond our control. We must learn how to accept them, and go along with our fate.

But by improving our outlook it is possible for us to keep a sincere and respectful heart, to reduce the mistakes in our words and actions, and ensure we treat others with courtesy and respect.

If you can make a good job of being yourself, then all over the world people will love and respect you like a brother.

Therefore, if you are a true, cultivated *junzi*, why grieve that you have no brothers?

These words, although they did not come from Confucius's own mouth, represent one of the values he advocates.

You must first be able to face squarely up to the regrets in your life, and to accept them in as short a time as possible. You must not get caught up in the middle of your regret, bewailing fate and asking why over and over again – this can only add to your pain.

Second, you must do as much as is possible to make up for this regret, by setting out to do the things you *can* do.

A single regret can become magnified out of all proportion. And what is the result? As the Indian poet

> This acknowledgement of the unsatisfactory parts of life, and ability to make up for these lacks through one's own efforts, is precisely the attitude with which Confucius tells us to approach the regrets in our lives.
>
> If a person cannot accept these regrets, what kind of consequences will this lead to in future?

Tagore said: 'If you shed tears when you miss the sun, you also miss the stars.'

In an old magazine I once read a story about a British tennis player, Gem Gilbert.

When she was small, Gem witnessed a tragedy. One day she went with her mother on a routine visit to the dentist. She thought that she and her mother would be home in no time. But something went very wrong indeed and the poor little girl watched her mother die in the dentist's chair.

This dark memory never left her and there seemed to be nothing she could do to erase it. But the one thing she could do was avoid ever going to the dentist herself.

Years later she became a wealthy and successful tennis player. One day she had such agonizing toothache that she could take no more. Her family eventually persuaded her she had to do something. 'Just get a dentist to come to the house. We don't have to go to the clinic, your doctor is here, we will stay with you, what's to be scared of?' And so they called a dentist to her home.

But something unexpected happened: after the dentist had set up his equipment and was preparing for surgery, he turned round to find that Gem Gilbert was dead.

This is the strength of psychological suggestion. A single regret can become so magnified that it hangs over you, affecting your whole life. If your life is haunted by regrets from which you cannot free yourself, these regrets can actually damage you physically as well as emotionally.

For example, in a certain small town there lived a very poor girl. She had lost her father, and she and her mother depended on each other for everything, scraping a meagre living from handicrafts. She suffered from terrible feelings

> Since it is impossible to avoid regrets in our lives, the attitude we adopt towards these regrets is extremely important. A different attitude can result in a completely different quality of life.

of inferiority, because she had never had any pretty clothes or trinkets to wear.

On the Christmas when she was eighteen, her mother did something she had never done before and gave her a purse of money, telling her to buy herself a present.

Such a treat was far beyond her wildest dreams, but she still lacked the courage to stroll naturally along. As she walked towards the shops, the purse clutched in her hand, she went out of her way to avoid the crowds, and stuck close to the wall.

On the way there she saw that all the people had better lives than her, and lamented to herself: I can't hold my head up here, I'm the shabbiest girl in this town. When she saw the young man she secretly admired more than any other, she wondered mournfully who his partner would be at the big dance to be held that night.

And so, creeping along and avoiding other people all the way, she reached the shop. As soon as she was inside, something caught her eye: a display of extremely pretty hair decorations.

While she was standing there in a daze, the shop assistant said to her: 'What lovely flaxen hair you have! Try a pale green flower to go with it, you'll look just beautiful.' She saw the price tag. It would have cost almost all her money and she said: 'I can't afford it, don't bother.'

But by then the shop assistant had already fastened that ornament to her hair.

The shop assistant brought a mirror and held it up to the girl. When she saw herself in the mirror, she was amazed. She had never seen herself like this, her face glowing with health and beauty; she felt as if the flower had transformed her into an angel! Without a moment's hesitation, she got out her money and bought it. Giddy with excitement in a way she had never felt before, she took her change, turned around and rushed outside, colliding with an old man who had just come in through the door. She thought that she heard him call out to her, but she was past worrying about all that, and hurtled out, her feet barely touching the ground.

Before she realized what she was doing, she had run all the way to the main street of the town. She saw that everyone was casting surprised glances in her direction, and she heard them discussing her, saying: 'I never knew there was such a pretty girl in this town. Whose daughter is she?' She met the boy she secretly liked again, and to her surprise he called out to her to stop, saying: 'Would you do me the honour of being my partner at the Christmas dance?'

The girl was wild with joy! She thought, I'll be extravagant for once – I'll go back and get myself a little something with the change. And with that, she flew elatedly back to the shop.

As soon as she came through the door, that old man said to her with a smile: 'I knew you'd be back! Just now when you bumped into me, your flower fell off. I've been waiting all this time for you to come back for it.'

This is where the story ends. The pretty hairslide had not really made up for all the sadness in the girl's life, but her new self-confidence made all the difference.

And where does self-confidence come from? It comes from a practical and steady sense of inner calm, an easy unhurried bearing that is the mark of the true *junzi*.

Confucius's student Sima Niu once asked him, what sort of person can be called a *junzi*?

Confucius replied: 'The *junzi* is free from worries and fears.'

Sima Niu asked again: 'So if someone has no worries or fears, he can be called a *junzi*?'

He perhaps thought that this standard was too low.

Confucius said: 'If he looks within himself, and sees nothing to make him ashamed or uneasy, of course there is nothing for him to worry about or to be afraid of.'

Today, we could use a common folk saying to interpret Confucius's meaning: 'If your conscience is clear, you won't be frightened by a midnight knock on your door.'

Arguably, reflecting on one's own conduct, and not being able to find anything to regret or be ashamed of could seem like quite a low standard. In some ways it is. Any one of us could do it. Equally, though, it could be rightly seen as the highest possible standard. Think about it: living so that every single thing we have ever done can stand up to scrutiny is a great challenge. That is why Confucius made it the standard for being a *junzi*.

How then do we achieve this sort of strong inner heart, which can help us live free from worry, indecision and fear?

If you want to achieve a strong inner heart, you must be indifferent to gains and losses, especially of the material kind. People who care too much about gains and losses were sometimes referred to by Confucius as 'the small man', and denounced as 'petty', in other words, small-minded and second-rate people.

Confucius once said: 'Can you let this kind of petty individual plan great matters of state?' No. When someone like this has failed to gain advantage, they complain about not being able to gain it; when they have got what they want, they are afraid of losing it. Since they are afraid of losing, they will stop at nothing to protect what they have and to try and gain more.

What is true courage? How does it differ from reckless foolhardiness? And what does Confucius have to say on the subject of courage?

A person who is obsessed with personal gains and losses can never have an open heart, or a calm, unperturbed mind, nor can they have true courage.

Confucius had a disciple called Zilu, a very impulsive man who cared a lot about matters of courage.

Confucius once said ironically: 'If one day my Great Way becomes unworkable, I will end up alone on a boat, floating on the seas and rivers. If anyone is still following me by then, it will probably be Zilu.'

Zilu was very pleased with himself when he heard this. But his teacher added: I say this because apart from courage, Zilu has nothing else. Love of courage was Zilu's defining quality, but his bravery was of the shallow, thoughtless kind.

But another day, Zilu asked his teacher: 'Does the *junzi* consider courage a supreme quality?'

Confucius said to him: 'For the *junzi* it is morality that is supreme. Possessed of courage but devoid of

> The Master said: 'In the eating of coarse rice and drinking of water, the using of one's elbow for a pillow, joy is to be found. Wealth and rank attained through immoral means have as much to do with me as passing clouds.' (*Analects* VII)

morality, a *junzi* will make trouble while a small man will be a brigand.'

What this means is that it is not wrong for a *junzi* to value courage, but it must be a controlled, restrained kind of courage; it has a precondition, which is 'morality'. Only bravery that puts morality first is true courage. Otherwise, a *junzi* could use their bravery to stir up trouble, and a petty person might even sink to becoming a robber.

If you think about it, robbers and bandits break into houses, commit robbery and even murder, but can you say that they are not brave? However, this bravery unrestrained by morality is the most harmful thing in the world.

So what is 'morality' and how do we know what is right and what is wrong?

It is clear that it is a kind of inner restraint. Confucius said: 'It is rare for a man to miss the mark through holding on to essentials!' (*Analects* IV) In other words, if a person has this inner restraint then they will make many fewer mistakes throughout their life.

If a person can truly manage to 'examine themselves on three counts' every day (*Analects* I), if you can truly reach the state in which 'when you meet someone better than yourself, you turn your thoughts to becoming his equal. When you meet someone not as good as you are, look within and examine your own self' (*Analects* IV), then you will have achieved restraint. To be able to reflect on one's own failings and work bravely to put them right, this is the true courage promoted by Confucius and his followers.

Many years later, the writer and statesman Su Shi described this bravery in 'On Staying Behind'. He called it 'great courage' and said:

What the ancients called a man of outstanding courage and talent must have self-restraint that surpasses that of ordinary men. There are things that humans cannot endure. When the ordinary man has been shamed, he draws his sword and rushes up to fight; this is not sufficient to be called bravery. There are those of great courage in the world, who when suddenly attacked are not afraid, when criticized without a reason do not become angry. This is because the ambitions of such men are great, and they cherish high and lofty aspirations.

As Su Shi saw it, the truly courageous had a 'restraint that surpasses that of ordinary men'. They could endure bitter public humiliation, just as the famous general Han Xin had faced public humiliation when he was forced to crawl between a man's legs in a public place rather than waste two lives in a duel to the death. This did not stop him from achieving remarkable successes in battle, winning a series of decisive victories. A man like him would never have reacted on a moment's brave impulse just for the sake of snatching a brief moment of satisfaction. This is because he possessed self-belief that was controlled by reason, and a settled, composed mind; this in turn is because he had a broad mind and high and lofty aspirations.

Su Shi described such a man as someone who 'when something unexpected happens they are not afraid'. This state of mind is very hard to achieve. We can try to be cultivated and moral people and not cause offence to others, but when others offend us for no reason at all, how can we stop ourselves becoming angry?

For example, if on Monday a man is victim of a sudden, severe and motiveless beating, on Tuesday he will describe it to all his friends, over and over again; by Wednesday he has sunk into a state of gloom and refuses to see anybody or go anywhere: by Thursday he starts to quarrel with his family over trifles . . .

What does this mean? It means that every time you retell the story you are beaten again. It means that even after the thing is past, you are still affected by it every day.

When misfortune approaches, the best way to deal with it is to let it pass as quickly as possible. Only in this way can you free more time to do the things that matter more, only then will you live more effectively, and be in better shape emotionally.

There are many things in our lives that are not as we would wish. Sometimes they are neither rational nor fair. We may lack the strength to change them, but we can change our own feelings and attitude. Looking at things in this way, we can say that people see whatever is in their heart. The following story of Su Shi and Foyin shows this.

As we have seen, Su Shi was a man of great achievements. Foyin was a high Buddhist monk, and the two of them often meditated together. Foyin was an honest, simple character, and Su Shi was always baiting him. Su Shi would often feel very pleased with himself over these small victories, and when he got home he liked to talk about them to his sister Su Xiaomei.

One day the two men were sitting meditating together.

Su Shi asked: 'Look, what do I look like?'

Foyin said: 'I think you look like a statue of the Buddha.'

When Su Shi heard this he laughed out loud, and said to Foyin: 'Do you know what I think you look like sitting there? Just like a pile of cow dung.'

Foyin was once again left at a loss for words.

When Su Shi went home he boasted about this to Su Xiaomei.

Su Xiaomei laughed coldly and said to her brother: 'How can you meditate with such low understanding? Do you know what people who meditate care about the most? It's all about seeing the heart and the essence: whatever there is in your heart will be there in your eyes. Foyin said you were like a Buddha, that shows that there is a Buddha in his heart; you said that Foyin was like a cowpat, so imagine what there must be in your heart!'

This can be applied to every one of us. Think about it: we all live on the same planet, but some people live warm, happy lives, and others moan and groan all day long. Are their lives really so different?

Actually, it is like half a bottle of wine. A pessimist would say: 'What a shame! Such a good bottle of wine and there's only half left!' while an optimist would say: 'How lovely! Such a good bottle of wine and there's still half left!' The only difference is in their attitudes.

In today's fiercely competitive society, it is more important now than at any other time in history to maintain a positive state of mind.

We should always remember that, as Confucius said, 'The *junzi* is at ease without being arrogant; the petty is arrogant without being at ease.' Because a *junzi*'s mind is calm, steady and brave, their serenity and wellbeing flow naturally from within; whereas what you see in a petty individual is a façade of haughtiness and self-importance; because their mind is restless and ill at ease.

Confucius once said: 'A man of benevolence never worries; a man of wisdom is never in two minds; a man of courage is never afraid.' (*Analects* XIV) But Confucius was also very modest. He said that these three things – never worrying, never being in two minds, and never being afraid – were things he had never achieved for himself.

What do we mean by 'A man of benevolence never worries'?

That is to say, somebody who has a great heart, full of benevolence and virtue, with an exceptionally kind, tolerant and generous spirit, will be able to overlook very many small details, and not make a fuss about trifles. Thus, he can avoid getting caught up in petty gains and losses. Only this kind of person can truly achieve inner peace and freedom from doubts and fears.

What is meant by 'A man of wisdom is never in two minds'?

Just fifty years ago, most Chinese might spend their entire life in just one work unit, divorce was almost unheard of, and they might well live in the same court-yard from childhood to old age. What troubled people was how predictable life was and what little choice there was.

But today we are troubled not by a lack of choice, but from too many choices. This bafflement and confusion is due to our vibrant, booming society.

We have no control over the external world; all we can do is improve our ability to make choices. When we have understood how to make those choices, how to accept or reject things, these worries and irritations will also cease to exist. This is what Confucius meant by 'A man of wisdom is never in two minds.'

But what is meant by 'A man of courage is never afraid'?

Putting it plainly, we might say: 'When two strong men come to blows, the bravest always comes out on top.' In other words, when you have sufficient courage and openness, you will be strong enough to move boldly forward, and then you will no longer be afraid.

When a true *junzi* achieves inner benevolence, wisdom and courage, then their worries, indecision and fear will all decrease as a result.

I once read a story in a book by the Japanese author Daisetsu Suzuki about a famous tea maker in the Edo period, who worked for a powerful and distinguished master. As we all know, Japan promotes the tea ceremony as a part of Zen, in which the tea ceremony and meditation are two parts of one whole.

One day the master decided to go to the capital on business. He could not bear to leave his tea maker behind, so he said to him: 'Come with me, so I can drink your tea every day.'

But Japan at that time was very dangerous. Bandits

and masterless samurai – ronin – roamed the countryside, terrorizing the inhabitants.

The tea maker was afraid. He said to his master: 'I have no skill with weapons, if I do run into trouble on the road, what will I do?'

His master said: 'Carry a sword and dress as a samurai.'

The tea maker had no choice. He changed into a samurai's clothes, and went with his master to the capital.

One day, the master had gone out to see to his business, so the tea maker went for a walk on his own. At that moment a ronin came up to him, and challenged him, saying: 'You're a warrior too, I see – let's try your skill against mine.'

The tea maker said: 'I don't know anything about fighting, I'm just a tea maker.'

The ronin said: 'You are not a samurai, but you're dressed as one. If you have any shame or self-respect at all, you should die by my blade!'

The tea maker racked his brains, but there was clearly no getting out of it, so he said: 'Spare me for a few hours so I can complete the tasks my master has given me. This afternoon we'll meet again by the pond.'

The ronin thought it over and agreed, adding: 'Be there, or else.'

The tea maker hurried straight to the most famous martial arts school in the capital. He went straight to the chief samurai and said to him: 'I beg you, teach me the most honourable way for a samurai to die!'

The chief samurai was extremely surprised. He said: 'People come here to seek a living, you're the first one to come seeking death. Why are you doing this?'

The tea maker described his meeting with the ronin, and then said: 'Making tea is all I know, but today I must engage in mortal combat with that man. I beg you to teach me how. All I want is to die with a little honour.'

The chief samurai said: 'Very well, you brew me some tea, and then I will tell you what to do.'

The tea maker was deeply distressed and said: 'This may be the last tea I prepare in this world.'

He did it with great concentration, calmly watching the mountain spring water come to the boil on the little stove, then putting in the tea leaves, washing the tea, filtering it and pouring it out, a little at a time. Then he took a cup in both hands and presented it to the chief samurai.

The chief samurai had been watching the entire process. He tasted a mouthful and said: 'This is the best tea I have drunk in my entire life. I can tell you right now that there is no need for you to die.'

The tea maker said: 'What will you teach me?'

The chief samurai said: 'There's no need for me to teach you anything. When you face that ronin, all you have to do is remember the state of mind you were in when you made the tea. You don't need anything else.'

After the tea maker had heard this he went to keep his appointment. The ronin was already waiting for him, and as soon as the tea maker arrived he drew his sword, saying: 'Now you're here, let the duel begin!'

The tea maker had been pondering the words of the great samurai all the way, so he faced this ronin in exactly the same state of mind as when he was brewing tea.

He fixed his gaze on his opponent, then unhurriedly removed his hat and placed it squarely beside him. Then he opened his loose outer robe, folded it slowly, and tucked it neatly under the hat; then he produced strips of cloth, and bound the sleeves of his inner garment firmly to his wrists; then he did the same to the cuffs of his trousers. He robed himself for battle from head to foot, remaining calm and unruffled throughout.

The ronin was getting anxious. The more he watched the more disconcerted he became, because he could not guess how great his opponent's skill with weapons really was. The look in the other man's eyes and his smile were making him increasingly unsure of himself.

When the tea maker had finished dressing himself, his final action was to draw his sword hissing from its scabbard, and brandish it in mid-air . . . and there he stopped, because he did not know what to do next.

At that moment the ronin threw himself to his knees, crying: 'Spare my life, I beg you! I have never seen so skilled a fighter in all my life!'

Was the tea maker's victory really thanks to his fighting skills? No, it was the bravery in his heart, and his relaxed, composed self-confidence. The attitude with which he approached his task.

Technique and skill are not what matter most. To fully comprehend those things that go beyond mere skill, we need to use our hearts and souls.

We can see that the standards of behaviour that Confucius has set us are not just an over-harsh critique of the world around us; they are about putting our limited time and energy to good use, and turning our criticism inwards towards our own hearts and minds.

We should all be a little stricter with ourselves, and a bit more honest and tolerant towards other people. These days we always say that a decent person should be honest and straightforward, but not in the sense of being naïve and too easily manipulated; instead what matters is the tolerance to forgive others' faults, treat them with compassion, and see things from that other person's point of view.

For this reason, only true *junzi* can manage 'not to blame heaven, nor to blame Man', neither complaining that Fate hasn't given them the lucky break they need, nor bewailing that there is nobody in the world who understands them.

A strong heart and soul can make up both for your innate, unavoidable regrets, and for the avoidable mistakes you make in life; at the same time it can give you fixity of purpose, raise your spirits, and let you live the fullest, most effective life possible. Every day you will experience a new rebirth, and you will show others the way to experience all these beautiful things.

If you are clear-headed and generous-minded, candid and brave, then you may find that you reap many unexpected benefits, and everybody will be willing to tell you all sorts of wonderful things. However, if you are the opposite of this, even a teacher such as Confucius, who taught worthy and unworthy alike, would not waste his breath talking to you.

As Confucius said, if you come across someone who could benefit from what you could tell them but you do not try to talk to them, you are 'letting a man go to waste'. You have missed your chance with that person, which is

> If a person's inner heart is free from worries, indecision and fear, they will naturally have fewer complaints about the world around them, and their ability to hold on to happiness will also increase.
>
> Increasing our ability to hold on to happiness is the greatest thing we can learn.

not good. Conversely, if this person refuses to listen, your words are going to waste, and this is not good either.

If you want to be the kind of person whom people are able to talk to, the key is to keep a clear and open mind. In our busy modern world, where society is ever more complex, it is vital that we adopt the broad-minded positive outlook of a *junzi*. Confucius shows us how.

Part Three

The Way of
the World

In the modern world, with email and messaging we can be constantly in touch with people thousands of miles away, yet we make no effort to get to know our neighbours.

More than ever before, the way we deal with other people is crucial.

In this confused and complicated social environment, how should we treat others?

When someone treats us unfairly how should we react? What are the principles we should adopt when dealing with the people closest to us?

Confucius gives us many rules on how to conduct our-selves in society and so be a decent person. These rules may at first appear fixed, even rigid, but in fact they contain a surprising flexibility.

Put simply, he gives us the principles that should govern our actions and the degree to which we should follow those principles.

We often ask ourselves what we should do and what we shouldn't; what is good and what bad.

Actually, when it comes to asking these questions, it very often happens that things cannot be divided accord-ing to simple ideas of right and wrong, good and bad, yes or no. When we do something, and the extent to which we do it, will also have a direct influence on how we should act. Confucius particularly stressed how far we should go in doing anything. Acting to excess or not doing enough are both to be avoided, as far as possible.

So, although Confucius advocated benevolence and

charity, he did not believe that we should pardon the faults of everybody we meet with indiscriminate benevolence. Somebody asked him: 'What do you think of the saying, "Repay an injury with a good turn"?'

Confucius replied: 'You repay an injury with straightness but you repay a good turn with a good turn.' This may not be quite what we would have expected to hear, but an awareness of the limits of what is acceptable in others is one key hallmark of the true *junzi*.

What Confucius is advocating here is respect for human dignity.

Of course, he did not suggest repaying one grievance with another grievance. If we constantly confront wrongs done to us with ill will and spite, then we will be caught up in a vicious circle that can never cease. We will sacrifice not only our own happiness, but our grandchildren's too.

Repaying a grievance with virtue is not practicable either. If you are too free with your goodness and mercy, treating those who have done you wrong with unnecessary kind-heartedness, this too is a waste.

But there is a third attitude, which is to face all of this calmly, with fair-mindedness, justice, openness and uprightness, that is to say, to approach it with a high moral character.

By extension, Confucius stressed that we must keep

our feelings and our talents for the places where they are needed.

These days everyone is trying to avoid wasting resources, yet we have overlooked the desolation of spirit and waste of energy that occurs within our own bodies every day.

Today's material prosperity and the increasing speed of the rhythms of life require us to make very swift judgements. We have to choose the best way to live, a way that is truly our own.

In our lives, we often see the following perplexing situations:

A father and mother who are good to their child, yet this only drives them away.

Friends who are as close as close can be, but always seem to end up hurting each other.

A person who schemes with all their might for a closer relationship with superiors and colleagues, yet who frequently achieves the very opposite.

How can this be?

Confucius believed that neither excessive aloofness nor excessive intimacy was ideal. For him 'going too far is as bad as not going far enough'. Extreme intimacy is not the ideal situation for two people who want to get along.

So how do we achieve 'good' relationships?

Confucius's student Ziyou said: 'To be importunate with one's lord will mean humiliation. To be importunate with one's friends will mean estrangement.' In other words, if you are always hanging around your superiors whether you have any business with them or not, although you are making a show of closeness you will soon bring humiliation upon yourself. Equally if you are always sticking close to your friend's side, although it appears that you are inseparable, estrangement will not be far away.

There is a fable that illustrates this. There once was a group of porcupines, all covered in sharp spines, huddling together to keep warm over the winter. They could never work out how far apart they should be. Just a little bit too far away and they couldn't keep each other warm, so they crowded closer; but as soon as they squeezed closer together, the sharp spines would prick them, so they started to move further apart, but once they did, they felt the cold. It took a good deal of trial and error for the porcupines to finally find the right degree of separation, so that they could retain the warmth of the group without hurting each other.

In China today, especially in the big cities, the old multi-family courtyards have all been pulled down and blocks of flats built in their place. Gone are the days when one family would make dumplings and give some to all the neighbours, and we no longer see all the inhabitants of a courtyard celebrate New Year together, one table for the adults, another for the children. Often neighbours who have lived for three or four years on the same staircase don't really know each other.

Because our relationships with the people who live around us have become colder, it is harder to for us to communicate with one another.

This then increases the burden on the few friends we do rely on.

You might think: My best friend should treat me a bit better, then I will go out of my way to be a bit nicer to him. You might think: If you're having family problems, a row with your partner, for example, why don't you tell me? I can step in and mediate for you!

A lot of us think in this way. But we should listen to Ziyou; excessive closeness is bound to harm other people.

So how should we get on with our friends?

Zigong once asked his teacher this question and

Confucius told him: 'Advise them to the best of your ability and guide them properly, but stop when there is no hope of success. Do not ask to be snubbed.' When you see a friend doing something wrong, you should do your best to warn them off, and guide them with good will, but if they really don't listen, let it go. Don't say any more, otherwise you're just making a rod for your own back.

So with good friends you also need boundaries. More is not always better.

Psychologists have a term for the kind of behaviour that we often see in modern people's interactions – 'non-loving behaviour'. It describes, very accurately, what happens when, in the name of love, people behave in a

> Confucius warns us that, whether with friends or leaders, we must keep a certain distance, and know where the boundaries lie between intimacy and estrangement.
>
> So, with our family, who are dearer to us than anyone else, should we be as close as close can be?
>
> Or should we also maintain a certain distance between parents and children, husband and wife, or between lovers?

grasping, coercive way towards those dearest to them. It often happens between husband and wife, between lovers, between mother and son, or father and daughter, in other words, between the people who are closest to one another.

A husband or wife might say to the other: 'Just look what I have given up for love of you. I did this or that just for the sake of this family, so now you must treat me a certain way.'

Lots of mothers say to their children: 'Look – after I had you, I fell behind at work, I lost my looks, I sacrificed everything for you, so why can't you do a bit better at school?'

All of this is non-loving behaviour: a sort of coercion in the name of love, to make other people behave the way we want them to.

I once read a book on parenting by a British psychologist, in which the author had some very wise things to say:

Love is almost always about bringing people closer together. But there is one kind of love, and one only, whose aim is separation: the love of parents for their children. Truly successful parental love means letting the child become independent and separate from your lives as early as possible; the earlier this separation, the more successful you have been as parents.

Seen like this, independence and a respectful distance are essential to an individual's personal dignity, and this respect should be maintained, even between the people we are closest to.

Whether between fathers and sons, mothers and daughters, or long-married husbands and wives, once that respectful distance is breached, once you have overstepped the mark, and reached the stage that Confucius calls 'importunate', so that you are no longer properly independent of each other, there will be problems. Hidden damage, estrangement or even a total breakdown in relations will not be far away.

Whether towards friends or family, we should all know where our limits are. Moderation is best.

So in our work life, is it really true that the more enthusiastic we are the better?

Is it the case that the more work we do, the better, whether it is part of our duty or not?

When dealing with work, are there also limits that we need to understand?

Confucius shows us that we must respect every person equally and rationally, maintain a tactful distance, and give each other breathing space.

This is very much like the Zen Buddhist state called 'the flower not fully open, the moon not fully round'.

This is the best state that can exist between people. As soon as a flower is fully open, it begins to fade; as soon as the moon is completely full, it immediately starts to wane. But when the flower is not fully open, nor the moon quite full, you will still feel anticipation, and have something to long for.

It is always like this, with both friends and family. By

The Master said: 'Have the firm faith to devote yourself to learning, and abide to the death in the good way. Enter not a state that is in peril; stay not in a state that is in danger. Show yourself when the Way prevails in the Empire, but hide yourself when it does not. It is a shameful matter to be poor and humble when the Way prevails in the state. Equally, it is a shameful matter to be rich and noble when the Way falls into disuse in the state.' (*Analects* VIII) giving them room you will find new horizons will open up in front of your eyes.

Many Chinese university students have done work experience in a foreign enterprise. As soon as you go in, the head of Human Resources will give you a written *job description*, which describes your position, and the job you will be doing. Everyone has one, from clerks and typists all the way up to the senior management.

In China, generally, we fix the type of work we do, but not how much. We are always saying that young people must work hard and well, and one person doing the work of three is the best of all, believing that this will help lighten the load for everyone. This is at odds with the spirit of modern enterprise management. The person responsible for a task should be the one to take care of it; in this way, everybody comes together as part of a coherent strategy.

Confucius said: 'Do not concern yourself with matters of government unless they are the responsibility of your office.' In other words, whatever position you are in, you must do your duty, you must not exceed your authority and meddle in other people's affairs, stepping beyond your remit to do things you don't have to do. This professional attitude to work is one to which our modern society in particular would do well to pay attention.

However, there is an implied condition here, which is: 'When they *are* the responsibility of your office, you *must* concern yourself with matters of government.' So then, when they are your responsibility, how should you concern yourself with matters of responsibility?

How do we know what we should do?

Confucius said: 'In his dealings with the world the *junzi* is not invariably for or against anything. He is on the side of what is moral.'

What Confucius meant was, the *junzi* doesn't try to force things, doesn't oppose things without a reason, is neither too demanding nor too detached, neither too close nor too distant, but acts morally and justly. Morality and justice should be the principles and standards by which we all conduct ourselves.

Once we know what should guide us in how we act, then we should concern ourselves with our actions themselves.

Between 'words' and 'actions', Confucius set greater store by 'actions'. He was extremely wary of people who brag and show off.

He said: 'It is rare, indeed, for a man with cunning words and an ingratiating face to be benevolent.' You cannot find someone of real virtue among the kind of people who are all fine words and an ingratiating manner.

So what did Confucius advocate? Very simply – say less, do more. You should be enthusiastic in your actions, but he advises 'cautious speech'. You must not say you can do something when you can't. As the Chinese folk saying goes, 'Troubles come from the mouth', and while this may be putting it a bit strongly, the least you can expect from boasts is 'too many words and you lose the meaning'.

Confucius's student Zizhang wanted to study in order to become an official.

Zizhang wanted a position of responsibility in society, and he asked his teacher what he should do. Confucius told him: 'Use your ears widely but leave out what is doubtful; repeat the rest with caution and you will make few mistakes. Use your eyes widely and leave out what is hazardous; put the rest into practice with caution and you will have few regrets. When in your speech you make few mistakes and in your action you have few regrets, an official career will follow as a matter of course.' (*Analects* 11)

'Use your ears widely but leave out what is doubtful' means that you must first use your ears and listen to what people are telling you, but the parts you aren't sure about you should leave to one side. We call learning from what happens to us direct experience, while learning from other people's experiences and the paths they have taken, including their frustrations and misfortunes, is called indirect experience.

'Repeat the rest with caution' means that you should be careful when you discuss what you have heard, even the parts that you think you are sure about. 'And you will have few regrets' means just that.

'Use your eyes widely and leave out what is hazardous' means look around you, but again leave things you aren't sure about to one side. Confusion is mostly the result of a limited field of vision: how can a frog at the bottom of a well understand the vastness of the ocean or the sky?

Once you have become rich in experience, you still have to be cautious in your actions. This kind of caution is described as behaving 'as if approaching a deep abyss, as if walking on thin ice.' (*Analects* VIII)

Think more, listen more, see more, be cautious in your words and in your actions – the advantage of doing things in this way is that you will have fewer regrets.

Nobody in the world sells a cure for regrets. As soon as a person knows they have done something wrong, the thing has become a fait accompli, and there is no way to retrieve it. If a person avoids placing blame and complaining when speaking, and in actions avoids many of the experiences that lead to regrets, they will be sure to succeed in what they set out to do.

There is a story I read on the internet.

Once there was a bad-tempered little boy, who was dreadfully stubborn, flying constantly into rages, smashing and hitting things. One day, his father took the child by the hand and led him to the fence at the back of their garden, saying: 'Son, from now on, every time you lose your temper at home, knock a nail into the fence. Then after a while you can see how many times you've lost your temper, all right?' The child thought, What's to be afraid of? I'll give it a try. After that, every time he threw a tantrum, he knocked a nail into the fence, and when he came a day later to look, he felt a bit embarrassed: 'Oh! All those nails! Heaps of them!'

His father said: 'Do you see? You have to control yourself. If you manage not to lose your temper for a whole day, you can pull out one of the nails from the fence.' The boy thought, If I lose my temper once then I have to hammer in a nail, but I have to go for a whole day without losing my temper before I can pull one out – that's really difficult! And yet, to get rid of the nails, he had to keep himself constantly under control.

At the start, the boy found it terribly difficult, but by the time he had pulled all the nails out of the fence, he suddenly realized that he had learned how to control himself. He went off happily to his father, saying: 'Daddy, quick, come and look, there are no more nails in the fence, and I don't lose my temper any more.'

The father went with the boy to stand next to the fence, and said in a voice full of significance: 'Look, son, the nails in the fence have all been pulled out, but the holes will stay there for ever. Every time you lose your temper with your family, it drives a hole into their hearts. When the nail has been pulled out, you can apologize, but you can never make the hole disappear.'

This story is a perfect explanation of what Confucius meant by 'in your speech you make few mistakes and in your action you have few regrets'.

When speaking, we must think carefully; in our actions, we must consider the consequences. This is the most important thing to remember in all our interactions..

If you want to be able to cope with all the different kinds of interpersonal relationships in our diverse and complex modern society, it is more important than ever to understand courtesy.

So how did Confucius understand courtesy?

Before we do a thing, we should pause for a moment to consider the consequences, just as once the nail is hammered in, even if it is pulled out later, the fence can never go back to the way it was before. When we do things, we must take the long view and be doubly cautious. In this way we can avoid hurting other people, and will have fewer regrets in the days to come.

Confucius set a great deal of store by ceremony in daily life. He respected courtesy, and observed the correct ceremonies, but never just for show, but as a kind of self-cultivation. When men who held official posts, people dressed in mourning and blind people went past, he would always stand up, even if the person was younger than him, and so below him in the social hierarchy. If he had to pass in front of these people, he would walk quickly, taking small steps, to show his respect.

This is courtesy.

Confucius behaved like this in other situations as well.

It is said of Confucius: 'When drinking at a village gathering, he left as soon as those carrying walking sticks had left.' 'When the villagers were exorcising evil spirits, he stood in his court robes on the eastern steps [the place for a host to stand].' When the wine-drinking ceremonies held by the villagers finished, Confucius always waited until the old people with walking sticks had gone through the door before leaving himself; he would never barge in front of them. When the country folk held a rite to drive out ghosts, Confucius always stood respectfully on the eastern steps, dressed in his court robes.

These are the very smallest of ceremonies. We might even wonder why the writers of the ancient books and records bothered to record a great sage doing such trivial things. Didn't everyone know to do this sort of thing? Isn't this just glorifying the sage?

Actually, the so-called sage's language and actions really were just that simple, so simple that it even makes people today a little bit suspicious. These stories are just like something that might happen in your neighbourhood, or in your home.

But how warm they are! It makes us feel that sages are not so far removed from us. Once again, Confucius shows us the truths he uncovered, and the events he experienced, for us to share.

We can therefore see that actions that may outwardly appear insignificant are truly important when they come from the heart and soul.

Confucius's student Zilu once asked his teacher how he could become a *junzi*. Confucius told Zilu: 'He culti-vates himself and thereby achieves reverence.' Cultivate yourself, and maintain a serious, respectful attitude. Zilu's reaction to this was: 'Just by doing this, you can become a *junzi*? Surely it can't be that simple?'

Confucius added a little more: 'He cultivates himself and thereby brings peace to his fellow men.' First make yourself a better person, then you can think of ways to make other people happy.

Zilu was plainly not satisfied with this, and pressed him further: 'Is that all?'

Confucius continued: 'He cultivates himself and thereby brings security to the people. Even Yao and Shun would have found the task of bringing peace and security to the people taxing.' Even *junzi* and sages such as Yao and Shun, the wise emperors of legend, would have found such a task hard going. If you can manage all this, you will certainly be good enough to be a *junzi*!

The Analects of Confucius is full of these simple little stories that might have happened to any one of us – we very rarely see any long sections of high-flown moralizing. We are not left feeling that the truths Confucius offers us are beyond our reach. Instead, they feel very warm, and within our grasp.

What Confucius tells us to focus on first is not how to bring stability to the world, but how to be the best possible version of ourselves. To 'cultivate one's moral character' is the first step towards taking responsibility for the nation, and for society. Confucius and his disciples struggled hard to be 'the best version' of themselves, but their aim in this was to better carry out their responsibilities to the society in which they lived.

Confucius said: 'Men of antiquity studied to improve themselves; men of today study to impress others.' (*Analects* XIV) The ancients studied in order to make themselves better people, but today we study in order to show off, and ingratiate ourselves with others.

Someone who has genuine respect for learning studies in order to improve his or her mind. Learning from books, learning from society, learning as we grow from childhood to old age, from all of this you will learn the ability to hold on to happiness.

First make yourself into a loyal, educated and knowledgeable citizen, then, armed with all this, go to find your place in society and your role in life. The aim of studying is to complete the process of finding your place and improving yourself.

And what is 'studying to impress others'?

It is the acquisition of knowledge as a mere tool, a skill that will help you get a job, or some other purely personal benefit.

Confucius never said that you have to be like any one person in order to be a *junzi*. As he saw it, to be a *junzi* is to be the best possible version of yourself, based on where you are right now, beginning with the things around you, and starting today, so that your mind can achieve a state of perfect balance. For it is only when you are possessed of a truly calm, steady, down-to-earth mind and heart that you can avoid being swayed by the rises and falls, gains and losses of life.

This reminds me of a little story:

Three tailors each opened a shop on the same street. Each of them wanted to attract the most customers.

The first tailor hung up a large sign, on which was written: 'I am the best tailor in the province.'

When the second tailor saw this he thought he would go one better, so he made a larger sign that read: 'I am the best tailor in the whole country.'

The third tailor thought: Am I supposed to say that I'm the best tailor in the whole world? He considered the matter for a very long time, and then put up a very small sign. It drew all the customers on the street to his shop, leaving the other two establishments deserted.

What did the third tailor's sign say? 'I am the best tailor in this street.'

He turned his eyes back to what was in front of him, starting out from the here and now. And this is why it was he who won the customers' approval.

> To do one's own work well and to be a good,
> kind person is the first requirement of a *junzi*.
> But is just being a good, kind person enough to
> make you a *junzi*? Not quite.

To be a good person, with heart and mind in perfect equilibrium, is a necessary condition of being a *junzi*. But this is not enough on its own. For Confucius, the *junzi* is not only good, he must also be a great and noble person, always mindful of the affairs of the world, and he must have real drive and energy.

China's ancient history is peopled by the natural successors of Confucius: famous scholars and intellectuals who lived in times of desperate hardship and poverty, yet never forgot the ordinary people.

At a time when his tumbledown thatched cottage with its leaky roof was barely enough to shelter him, the poet and sage Du Fu: wrote: 'How can I get a hundred thousand mansions, to shelter all the poor people of the world and bring smiles to their faces?' In other words, despite his own poor dwelling, he wanted everyone who was without a decent home to have one. Reading his words today, we feel that this is no idle boast on Du Fu's part. Instead, we are moved by his generosity of spirit.

To give another example, the poet, Fan Zhongyan believed that whether a *junzi* was 'inhabiting the heights of the temples and halls of official life' or 'situated amidst the far lakes and rivers', he should nevertheless feel concern both for the rulers of his country and for the common people of the world, and so 'be the first to worry for the worries of the world, and the last to take joy in the joys of the world'.

The influence of Confucius can clearly be seen in the poet's words.

At this point, you might begin to wonder if the Confucian idea that 'the nation is my responsibility' must inevitably mean the sacrifice of one's own personal interests.

Actually Confucius did not advocate such a sacrifice. On the contrary, his calm, warm, practical theory of human relations suggests that to do as much for society as your abilities allow is the greatest possible protection of the rights and benefits of all.

However, Confucius believed that when seeking personal advantage you must not stray from the correct path, nor must you constantly seek short cuts or petty victories.

> The Master said: 'There are three things constantly on the lips of the gentleman, none of which I have succeeded in following: 'A man of benevolence never worries; a man of wisdom is never in two minds; a man of courage is never afraid.' Tzu-kung said: 'What the Master has just quoted is a description of himself.' (*Analects* XIV)

Confucius maintained that the difference between the *junzi* and the petty was whether they took the correct path or took short cuts.

He said: 'The *junzi* understands what is moral. The petty understands what is profitable.' (*Analects* IV) The Chinese word *yi*, here translated as moral, sounds the same as another character, which means 'appropriate' or 'suitable'. That is to say, the road that the *junzi* takes is the truest and most appropriate path from its beginning to its end. A petty individual, on the other hand, concentrates on personal advantage, and pursuing that advantage, it is very easy for them to fall into evil ways.

So how do the differences between a *junzi* and a petty person show themselves?

Confucius said: 'While the *junzi* cherishes benign rule, the small man cherishes his native land. While the *junzi* cherishes a respect for the law, the small man cherishes generous treatment.' In other words, a *junzi* does not have the same daily concerns as the petty person.

Not a day goes by without a *junzi* thinking about morality and self-cultivation, while a small-minded person considers only their own immediate circumstances - their home or their personal needs and desires. The *junzi* always live by the rules of a strict moral code, which cannot be broken, while petty people fill their heads with thoughts of trivial favours and how they can get the upper hand.

Someone who spends their days preoccupied with the affairs of their own family, such as how they can buy a flat or climb the career ladder, who is full of little schemes to improve their family's lifestyle, is the kind of petty individual that Confucius was talking about. Of course there is nothing terribly wrong with this, but if someone allows their heart to become a prisoner as they scrabble for these scraps of personal advantage, if they discard the restraints of morality or the law in order to protect or expand such tiny advantages, then it can be very dangerous.

The *junzi* has always respected morality and the law. It's just like any one of us when we take the footbridge over a busy road, or wait for the lights at a pedestrian crossing: these acts may seem to be a restriction upon us, but these little restrictions, when they guarantee our safety, actually show mutual respect and enhance society.

Petty people, who are greedy for immediate gain, who use little loopholes and take small advantages, may get what they want once or twice, but there is a potential danger hidden there, and they're certain to come off the worse for it sooner or later. Let's take crossing the road again: as soon as a petty person sees the traffic lights are about to change, without waiting for the pedestrian signal, they rush across, thinking that by doing so they are getting in first, but we know very well what will happen sooner or later.

A petty person doesn't look at things in the right way, but is always eager to snatch small advantages.

In today's society, what can we do to become a *junzi*? We can start with the idea of 'perseverance' or constancy. As young adults, we are all idealistic, full of ambition and hopes of achieving something useful. But why are these ambitions so often unfulfilled? In modern life we are faced with many complex choices, and with all this excitement and stimulation, it is hard for us to make decisions as we waver between a multitude of choices. We find it impossible to choose which path to take to achieve our ambitions. And this shows lack of 'perseverance'.

If we really persevere and learn to take the long

view, even if we haven't reached the exalted state of those Confucius describes as having 'no fixed abode but a fixed heart', being concerned more with what is inside us than with our external life, then we are well on the way to being a *junzi*.

There is a second standard for a *junzi*, which is: 'The *junzi* is conscious of his own superiority without being contentious, and comes together with other *junzi* without forming cliques.' (*Analects* xv)

In other words, a *junzi* is sociable and gets on well with others. But nothing can undermine their inner dignity; they are never competitive with those around them. Neither would a *junzi* ever form cliques or scheme for personal advantage.

This is what Confucius means when he says: 'The *junzi* agrees with others without being an echo.' (*Analects* xiii)

In any large group of people, everybody's personal convictions will never be exactly the same, but a true *junzi* will listen earnestly as each person states their own point of view and will be able to understand and respect the logic of everyone's ideas, while at the same time holding fast to their own. This maintains both unity and harmony, while ensuring that everyone's voice is heard. These days, when we in China say that we want to build up a Harmonious Society, this means taking everybody's different voices and harmoniously blending them into the voice of the greater collective.

Petty people are exactly the opposite, they 'echo without being in agreement.' (*Analects* XIII)

> The Master said: 'The gentleman agrees with others without being an echo. The small man echoes without being in agreement.'
> (*Analects* XIII)

We have all come across situations at work, say, or at school, or college, when an issue is being discussed and the boss says something. Before the words are properly out of their mouth, someone will immediately jump up and sycophantically say: 'Yes, yes, my goodness yes, how right you are!', really laying it on with a trowel: 'What a brilliant idea!' But as soon as the meeting is over, they turn to someone else and say: 'What's that man on about this time? I don't agree with him at all!'

Confucius gives another description of the ways in which the *junzi* and the petty behave very differently: 'The *junzi* enters into associations but not cliques; the small man enters into cliques but not associations.' (*Analects* II)

Junzi 'enter into associations' with others who like them have high standards of morality and justice, which they use in their dealings with others, so they have many friends who cherish the same ideas and follow the same path. No matter how many friends a true *junzi* has, they will always be like oxygen in the air we breathe, making their friends feel happy and cared for. The Chinese character, 比, for 'enter into cliques' looks like two people standing close together. This means that petty people prefer to get together in their own little cliques, they don't like to be absorbed into the big collective.

For example, at a party a *junzi* will feel completely at ease with everyone there, whether old friends or strangers; but a petty person will skulk in a corner with their best friend, the two of them muttering away to each other, as thick as thieves.

Why are there such differences between people? Again, it is because the *junzi* and the petty do not exist in the same moral state. Confucius said: 'The *junzi* is easy of mind, while the small man is always full of anxiety.' (*Analects* VII) The reason why the petty are often found conspiring with others is that they have an uneasy conscience, and want to plot for their own advantage and protect what they already have. When we talk about cronyism or forming cliques this is exactly what we mean. The mind of the *junzi*, on the other hand, is contented and composed; because he or she is in a state of peaceful ease without selfishness, and can be placid, and come together with others in a kind, friendly way.

In China, we have always regarded harmony as a thing of beauty, but what is true harmony? Confucius repeatedly shows us it is a tolerance towards others, a kind of melding and mingling, all the while maintaining different voices and different viewpoints. This is the way of the *junzi* in society.

Because there are so many differences between a *junzi* and a petty individual, you will find your dealings with them will be very different.

Confucius said: 'The *junzi* is easy to serve but difficult to please. He will not be pleased unless you try to please him by following the Way, but when it comes to employing the services of others, he does so within the limits of their capacity. The small man is difficult to serve but easy to please. He will be pleased even though you try to please him by not following the Way, but when it comes to employing the services of others, he demands all-round perfection.' (*Analects* xiii)

Confucius explains these differences in a way that is extremely easy to understand, because he always puts the *junzi* and the petty side by side in order to compare them.

It is very easy to get along with a *junzi*, but you will

find it very hard to ingratiate yourself with one. If you want to please them using underhand means, they will not be at all pleased. They would never agree to wave you through ahead of others, or throw open the back door in exchange for small favours. But by the time they actually make use of you, they will have arranged a suitable place for you, based on your talents and abilities. This is what is meant by 'within the limits of their capacity'.

The defining characteristic of petty people is that it is very easy to suck up to them, but it is very hard to work alongside them. For example, if you do them a few small favours, or help them in some small way, even wine and dine them, this person will be very happy. Even if your way of pleasing them is not strictly moral, or even actually dishonest, they will still be very happy. But this kind of person is also rather difficult to work with. Don't ever think that once you've managed to get on their good side they will loyally smooth your path: even if you've put in a lot of effort, and spent a lot of money to buy them off, by the time they really want to employ someone, they will not arrange a job for you based on your talent and ability, but will demand perfection, and complain that you are not up to the mark here, haven't made the grade there, and all your efforts will have gone to waste. They will find ways to make things difficult for you, and put you in very awkward positions. Working with someone like this is very hard going.

Somebody once asked Zilu: 'What kind of man is your teacher Confucius?' Zilu did not reply. Later, Confucius said to Zilu: 'Why didn't you reply: "He is the sort of man who forgets to eat when he tries to solve a problem that has been driving him to distraction, who is so of full of joy that he forgets his worries and who does not notice the onset of old age."'

This is in fact a portrait of Confucius, and also of the moral character that all Chinese intellectuals hoped to attain.

When it comes down to it, the aim of Confucian philosophy was to nurture those we might call followers of the Way of Confucius. In other words, its aim was to educate an elite class of scholar-officials whose primary mission was to serve their country and their culture.

In his poem 'Memorial to Yueyang Tower', Fan Zhongyan describes the essence of this role as: 'Be the first to worry for the worries of the world, and the last to take joy in the joys of the world.' For him, it meant forgetting all about personal gains and losses, and absorbing yourself in the interests of the greater collective.

But once again we see that this profound conviction and sense of responsibility to society is founded on plain, simple things, and begins in the here and now. The starting point is in the cultivations of one's self, so that we become the best possible version of who we are.

That way, when, as often happens, we hear people complain that society is unfair, and that it is hard to deal with the world around us, rather than moaning about our fate or blaming other people, we do better to look inwards and examine ourselves. If we can manage to fully understand where our limits lie, to be cautious and circumspect in our words and actions, to bring the spirit of Confucian courtesy and honour to the world, and to develop our mind and body, we will have many fewer things to trouble us, and so we will come to understand how to be a good person and how best to deal with the world.

I don't think such moral ambition is merely something to read about in the past. It is a way of living that every one of us can practise, now, in the twenty-first century, and we can begin today. That way, the happiness that Confucius and his disciples enjoyed can be a wellspring of happiness for us today. This is probably the greatest lesson that Confucius *can* give us, and his greatest gift.

If we have an optimistic and positive attitude, and a proper understanding of the boundaries and limitations of dealing with others, we can become the kind of person who brings happiness to others, and let our own happiness become a source of energy, shining like the sun on those around us, bringing comfort to our family and friends and even, eventually, to the whole of society. But, as *junzi*, we must begin with our friends.

Part Four

The Way of
Friendship

Of all the relationships we have, it is our friends who most directly reveal the kind of person we are.

If you want to understand someone, you only have to look at their circle of friends, which will tell you what their values and priorities are – after all, as is often shown, birds of a feather flock together.

But friends are divided into good and bad. The right sort of friend can help you a lot, but the bad sort will bring you a great deal of trouble, and may even lead you down the wrong road. Being able to choose your friends wisely is extremely important.

So what kind of friend is a good friend? What kind of friend is a bad friend? How can we make good friends?

Confucius attached a great deal of importance to the effect of friends on a person's development. He taught his own students to make good friends, and to avoid bad ones.

He said that there are three types of friends in this world who can help us.

The first are straight friends. Straight here means upright, honest, and fair-minded.

A straight friend is sincere and great-hearted, he or she has a kind of bright, transparent openness about them, without a trace of flattery. Their character will have a good influence on your own. They will give you courage when you are timid, and decisiveness and resolution when you are wavering.

The second are friends who are loyal and trustworthy.

This friend is honest and sincere in his or her dealings with others, and is never fake. Associating with this kind of friend makes us feel calm, composed and safe, they purify and elevate our spirits.

The third is the well-informed friend. This kind of friend is possessed of a great deal of knowledge about a great many things and has seen a lot of the world.

The pre-Qin period (before 221 BC) when Confucius lived was quite different from today, with our computers, Internet, sophisticated information resources and all our different kinds of media. In those days, what did people do when they wanted to widen their outlook? The easiest way was to make a well-informed friend, absorbing the books he or she had read and all their experience into your own direct experience.

When you find yourself dithering over a problem, unable to come to a decision, you would be well advised to go to see a well-informed friend. That friend's wide-

> The three kinds of beneficial friends are true friends, loyal friends and well-informed friends.
>
> Confucius also said that there are three sorts of bad friends: 'He stands to lose who make friends with three other kinds of people.' So what sort of people are these?

ranging knowledge and experience will help you with your choice.

Having a well-informed friend is like owning a huge encyclopedia; we can learn many useful lessons from their experiences.

Confucius said that there are three kinds of bad friends, 'the ingratiating in action, the pleasant in appearance and the plausible in speech', and that to have these three types as friends is 'to lose'. So how can we tell what kind of people they are?

By the 'ingratiating in action', Confucius meant flatterers and fawners – shameless toadies.

We often encounter this sort of person in our lives. No matter what you say, they will always say: 'That's just so brilliant'; whatever you do, they will always say: 'That's amazing.' They will never say 'No' to you. On the contrary they will slavishly follow you and take their tone from yours, praising you and paying you compliments.

This kind of friend has a talent for weighing your words and watching your expressions. They trim their sails to suit the wind, making sure they never do anything that they sense might displease you.

They are the absolute opposite to the good straight friend. The hearts of these people are neither straightforward nor honest, and they have no sense of right and wrong. Their aim is to make you happy, but only so that they can get something out of it.

Most Chinese people have heard of the treacherous minister He Shen, a character in the TV series *Iron Teeth, Copper Teeth*. This man fawns on the Qianlong Emperor in every possible way. He is the worst kind of sycophant and there's almost nothing he won't stoop to. He is a classic example of this type of bad friend.

A friend like this will make you feel unusually comfortable and happy, just like the Qianlong Emperor in the TV series: he knew very well that He Shen was taking bribes and perverting the law, but even so he could not bear to be without him. As Confucius says, making friends with this kind of person is extremely dangerous!

Why?

After being told all the things you want to hear, and flattered into a state of contentment, it will start to go to your head; your ego will swell uncontrollably and you will become blindly self-important, caring for nobody but yourself. You will lose the most basic capacity for self-knowledge, and it will not be long before you bring down disaster on your own head.

This kind of friend is slow poison for the soul.

The second harmful friend is the person that Confucius called 'the pleasant in appearance', or two-faced.

They will be all smiles and sweetness to your face, positively beaming as they dish out their compliments and flattery; they are precisely what Confucius meant by 'a man with cunning words and an ingratiating face'. But behind your back they will spread rumours and malicious slander.

We often hear people complain: 'That friend of mine seemed so kind and loving, his speech was so gentle, his behaviour so thoughtful, I believed he was my closest, most intimate friend, I was genuinely committed to helping him, I poured out my heart to him too, told him my innermost secrets. But he betrayed me, abusing my trust for his own ends; he started rumours about me, spread my secrets, destroyed my character. And then when I confronted him, he had the gall to deny it to my face, and put on a show of injured innocence.'

This kind of person is false and hypocritical, the exact opposite of the frankness and honesty of the loyal and trustworthy friend.

People like this are the true 'petty people' – petty, and with a dark shadow in their hearts.

However, such people often wear a mask of goodness. Because they have an ulterior motive, they will be very friendly towards you; they might be ten times nicer to you than somebody with no hidden agenda. So if you aren't careful and let yourself get used by this person, you will find that you have fitted shackles to your own wrists: this friend will not let you go unless you pay a heavy price. This is a test of our judgement, and of our understanding of people and the ways of the world.

The third kind Confucius called 'the plausible in speech', referring to people who brag and exaggerate. Ordinary people might call them 'fast talkers'.

There is nothing this kind of person doesn't know, and no argument they don't understand. They talk in an endless stream, carrying you along with their momentum until you can't help believing them. But in actual fact, apart from the gift of the gab, they have nothing else at all.

There is a clear difference between the kind of person described above and 'the well-informed', which is that this kind of person has no real talent or knowledge. A person who is plausible in speech has a glib tongue, but nothing inside to back it up.

Confucius was always suspicious of glib people and their sweet words. A *junzi* should speak less and do more. Confucius believed that it is not what a person says that matters, but what they do.

Of course, in modern society there has been a change in attitudes and values: if people with real talent and true scholarship cannot communicate effectively and do not get their meaning across, it will obstruct their careers – and their lives.

However, if someone can only talk, and has no real skill, it is something far more harmful.

> The three harmful friends found in *The Analects of Confucius* are flattering friends, two-faced friends and big-talking friends. On no account make friends with this sort of person, or else you will end up paying a painful price.
>
> But, whether a person is good or bad is not written on their face. How can we make good friends and steer well clear of bad friends?

If you want to make good friends, and avoid making bad, you need two things: the first is the desire to make good friends, the second is the ability to do so. We have already seen how important 'benevolence' and 'wisdom' are, and they are key if we wish to make good friends. The desire to make good friends comes from benevolence and the ability to make them from wisdom. As you will remember, when Fan Chi asked his teacher what he meant by benevolence, his teacher answered with only two words: 'Loving people.'

Fan Chi then asked, then what is this thing called wisdom?

The teacher replied, again with just two words: 'Knowing people.' To understand others is to be wise.

Plainly, if we want to make good friends, we must first have a kind, benevolent heart, be willing to get close to people, and have the desire to make friends; second, we must have the ability to discriminate. Only in this way can one make friends of real value. Once you have this basic standard, you will be well on your way to making friends of the very best kind.

In a sense, making a good friend is the beginning of a beautiful new chapter in our lives. Our friends are like a mirror: by watching them, we can see where we ourselves fall short.

However, there are some thoughtless people who spend almost all their time with their friends, but never seem able to make these comparisons.

I'll give you a perfect example of someone who couldn't. The sixty-second volume of China's great history, *Records of the Grand Historian*, tells the story of Yanzi, the famous prime minister of the Kingdom of Qi.

As everyone in China knows, Yanzi was short and

> Confucius said: 'He stands to benefit who makes friends with three kinds of people. Equally, he stands to lose who makes friends with three other kinds of people.
>
> To make friends with the straight, the trustworthy and the well-informed is to benefit. To make friends with the ingratiating, the pleasant in appearance and the plausible in speech is to lose.'

stumpy-limbed, with a plain, unremarkable face and rather coarse features. But he had a very handsome, tall, dashing charioteer.

This charioteer, funnily enough, thought that it was a very splendid thing to drive the chariot of the prime minister of the Kingdom of Qi. He was very proud of his position: every day sitting at the front of the chariot, whipping on the tall horses, while Yanzi had to sit behind in the covered part. He thought that his job as a charioteer was just the best thing ever!

One day, the charioteer came home to find his wife packing her bags, weeping bitterly. He asked in surprise: 'What are you doing?' His wife replied: 'I can't take any more, I'm leaving you. I'm ashamed to live with you.'

The charioteer was astonished: 'But don't you think

I'm splendid?' His wife retorted: 'What do you think splendid *is*? Look at Yan Ying, a talented man who's in charge of the whole country, yet he's so modest, sitting in the chariot without the least fuss or show. You're just a driver, but you think there's no end to your own splendour, strutting about with a high and mighty expression written all over your face! You spend all day with a man like Yan Ying, but you don't have the wit to learn anything at all from him to reflect on yourself – that's what has made me despair of you. Living with you is the most shameful thing in my life.'

Eventually, Yan Ying heard about what had happened and said to his driver: 'Since you have such a good wife, I should give you a better position.' And he promoted the charioteer.

This story tells us that all the people around us, their ways of living and their attitudes in dealing with the world, can become a mirror for us. The key is to keep our wits about us.

The beneficial friends of whom Confucius approved are those who are useful to us. But by useful we do not mean to say that this friend will be able to help you get on in the world, on the contrary, Confucius never advocated taking up with rich or powerful people. Instead, he favoured making friends with people who can perfect your moral character, increase your self-cultivation and enrich your inner self.

In classical Chinese there is a school of pastoral poetry. Poets of this school were notable for their desire to retreat from society, live in seclusion and commune with the natural world, and their work praises the joys of nature and a simple, rural life.

So where can we find this communion with nature? It is not deep in the wild mountains and forests, but in real life. It has been said that 'it is easier to find solitude in the market place than in the wilderness'. Only a recluse who had not yet perfected their ability to cultivate themselves would hide away up a mountain, and affectedly build themselves a country retreat there; a true hermit has no need to retreat from the mundane world, but can live in the heart of a noisy, bustling city, doing things that are not the slightest bit different from everybody else, and differing from other people only in a certain inner calm and steadiness.

Everyone in China knows Tao Yuanming, one of the first recluses who, as we saw in Part One, would never compromise his ideals, and who became the founder of the pastoral school of poetry. Tao Yuanming lived in rather straitened circumstances, but he had a very happy life. The *Southern Histories* tell us that Tao Yuanming had no knowledge of music, but he owned a zither. This zither was just a big length of wood, it did not even have any strings. Every time he invited his friends to his house, he would stroke the piece of wood, saying that he was playing the zither, and he would pour all his heart into his playing, sometimes playing for hours until he was weeping audibly. And every time he did this, those friends who really understood music were also visibly moved. Tao Yuanming would play out the music of his soul on his stringless zither, while his friends drank wine and talked happily among themselves. Afterwards, he would say: 'I am drunk and I want to sleep, you may go.' The friends left without making a fuss, and continued to meet on similar occasions in the future. Friends like this are true friends, because your souls share an unspoken understanding. And this kind of life is truly happy.

Make friends who are happy, and can take pleasure in their lives the way they are right now.

I once read an essay by the famous Taiwanese writer Lin Qingxuan, about a friend who asked him for a piece of calligraphy to hang in his study. The friend said to him: 'Write me something that is extremely simple, but which will be helpful to me when I see it every day.' He thought for a long time, and then wrote just four Chinese characters: 'Think Often of One and Two.' That friend did not understand, and asked what it meant. Lin Qingxuan said: 'We all know the saying that "Out of every ten things in this world eight or nine will not go as I wish; and there is a mere handful of people I can communicate with." Supposing we accept this, there will still be at least one or two things out of every ten that *do* go as we wish. I can't help you too much, all I can do is to tell you to think of those "one or two" things, to turn your mind to happy things, to magnify the light of happiness, to keep the sadness in your heart at bay. As a friend, this is the best thing I can do for you.'

There is a Western fable about a king who led a life of luxury and splendour, full of wine, women, music and adventure; all the most beautiful and precious things in the world were his to command, but still he was not happy. Neither did he know what would make him happy, so he had his attendants summon his personal physician.

The doctor examined him for a long time, and then prescribed a cure: 'Have your people search the kingdom for the happiest person in it. Wear his shirt, and it will make you happy.'

So the king sent his ministers off to search for that person, and finally they found a genuinely happy man, incurably happy, in fact. But the ministers reported that they had been unable to bring back the man's shirt for the king to wear.

The king said: 'How can that be? You have to bring me that shirt!'

The ministers said: 'That man is a pauper and always goes about bare-chested – he doesn't even own a shirt.'

This reminds us that in life true happiness is happiness of the soul, and does not necessarily have a very strong connection with external, material living conditions. Confucius lived in a time of considerable material poverty, and in his time the strength of true happiness came from a rich inner life, from behaving in the right way and from ambitions and desires, but also from good friends who learned from each other.

Having once come to understand what a good friend is, we also need to know how to get on well with them. Does having a good friend imply that we must be permanently joined together at the hip? In China, we often say of two people that they are so close that they wear just one pair of trousers between them. But is this an appropriate closeness for friends?

Everything that lacks proportion or proper limits in this world will end up going too far, which, as we know, is as bad as not going far enough. Equally, when dealing with friends, we have to pay attention to boundaries. For example when you make friends with a *junzi*, you need to know when to speak and when not to speak and to know how far you can reasonably go.

Confucius said: 'When one is in attendance on a *junzi*, one is liable to three errors. To speak before being spoken to by the *junzi* is rash; not to speak when being spoken to by him is to be evasive; to speak without observing the expression on his face is to be blind.' (*Analects* XVI)

Jumping up and stating your views before a conversation has had a chance to get anywhere is rash and insensitive, which is not a good thing. We all have our own particular interests, but you should wait until the time is ripe, when your chosen subject has become the focus of general attention and everyone is waiting to hear about it, and only then, and without undue haste, say your piece.

Many people now have their own blogs, or use websites in which they eagerly display their innermost hearts for all to see. But in the past there were no such blogs, and everybody depended on the spoken word to understand one another and to communicate. When we get together with friends, there will always a few people who go on and on about their own affairs: I was out playing golf the other day, I've just been promoted, and so on and so forth. Or when some women get together, there may be one who pushes herself forward to regale us with endless details of her husband and children. Of course, these are all things that she wants very much to say, but does everybody care about these things? That is to say, while she is the only one doing the talking, she strips away the rights of other people to choose a topic. To jump in with both feet and insist on saying your piece before the right time has come is certainly not good.

But there is another extreme: 'not speaking when being spoken to'. Confucius called this fault 'being evasive'.

In other words, the conversation has naturally reached a point where you should be the one to take the conversation further, but you drag your feet, and refuse to speak your mind. This kind of friend leaves everyone feeling excluded. Since the topic has already come this far, why don't you say anything? Is it self-protection? Are you deliberately holding yourself aloof? Or are you trying to whet our appetite? In short, keeping silent when you should speak is not good either.

The third kind of situation is characterized by Confucius as 'to speak without observing the expression on his face is to be blind', which is what we would today call an inability to read people.

'Blind' in this context is a great criticism. A person who gets up to speak without watching other people's expressions is a social illiterate. You must be careful to understand the person you are talking to, you should look to see what words can be said, and what is better left unsaid. This is the tactful respect that should always exist between friends.

And not just friends. There should be tactful avoidance of certain painful issues even between husband and wife, father and son. The life of every adult contains both private triumphs and private miseries, a true friend must not lightly touch on another's private pains, and for that, you need to be able to read people. Of course, this is not a kind of slavish pandering to other people's tastes. Rather, it creates a peaceful, friendly atmosphere for you and your friends, so that you can communicate freely.

There is a famous example of this.

The actress Vivien Leigh shot to fame with the Hollywood film *Gone with the Wind*, which won ten Oscars. This film was an immediate hit, and at the height of its fame she went on tour to Europe for the first time.

Everywhere she went, thousands of journalists clustered eagerly around as Leigh's private plane touched down on the runway.

But one journalist, who lacked this ability to read people, pushed his way to the front and eagerly addressed a question to Leigh, who had just alighted: 'Tell me, miss, what part did you play in this film?' At this question, Leigh turned on her heel, went back inside the plane and refused to come out again.

Is asking a question like this in a situation you know nothing about so very different from being blind?

Apart from that, when offering friends advice, or giving them warnings, even if your intentions are good, you must be able to understand how far you can go.

Confucius said to Zigong that when giving advice, you must 'Advise them to the best of your ability and guide them properly, but stop when there is no hope of success. Do not ask to be snubbed.' (*Analects* XII) That is, you don't necessarily have to be like a dose of bitter medicine, you don't have to smack them round the head and shout in their ear. It is perfectly possible for you to say what you have to in a pleasant but persuasive manner. This is 'guiding them properly'. If you can't get through to them, let it go at that. Don't wait until they lose patience with you, and don't go courting embarrassment.

Whatever you do, you can't just order people to do as you say. Today, not even mothers can expect that of their own children. Every individual is worthy of respect, and friends particularly must maintain mutual respect. Give them the right advice, or a proper warning, do your duty and no more; this is what good friends are for.

> People make different friends in different stages of life. How do we make the friends that are best suited to us at each stage?

Confucius said that seventy or eighty years of human life seem to be a long time, but it can be divided into three distinct stages: youth, maturity and old age. In every stage there are things that we need to be particularly careful about, which we sometimes call pitfalls. If you can manage to get past all three of these pitfalls, then you will encounter no other serious obstacles in your life. And to overcome these three sets of pitfalls, we can't do without the help of our friends.

Confucius said: 'In youth when the blood and *qi*, or life force, are still unsettled he should guard against the attraction of feminine beauty.' Young people are very prone to impulsive behaviour, and they should make sure to avoid romantic difficulties. We often see high school and university students troubled by emotional problems. At this time of life, a good friend acts as an onlooker, who sees things more objectively and clearly, so they can offer solutions to the knotty problems we cannot untie ourselves.

When this pitfall is past, we arrive at middle age. Confucius said of this stage: 'When the blood and *qi* have become unyielding, he should guard against bellicosity.'

When people reach middle age, their family life is stable and they are established in their profession, so what is most on their mind at this time? The desire to make space for themselves, to expand their domain. However, this is all too liable to cause contradictions and conflicts with others, and both sides may very well come off worse as a result. So Confucius warns us that the most important thing for people in mid-life is to caution against getting involved in conflicts. Rather than fighting with other people, it is better to struggle with oneself, and try to find ways to improve. If, in the end, you miss out on that promotion, you should ask yourself whether it might not be because you could have done better in some way.

In this period, therefore, you should make friends with people who are calm and matter-of-fact. They will help you take the long view of temporary victories and defeats, overcome the temptations of material things, obtain spiritual comfort, and find a place of repose and respite for the soul.

But what should we beware of when we arrive in our later years? According to Confucius, 'When the blood and *qi* have declined, he should guard against acquisitiveness.'

In old age, people's minds show a tendency to slow down and become more tranquil. The philosopher Bertrand Russell compared this stage to a rapidly flowing river that rushes headlong through the mountains, but by the time it finally merges with the sea has become slow, broad and placid. At this stage of life, people should have learned how to deal with possessions and achievements in a sensible way.

When young, we all live a life of addition, but after reaching a certain point, we have to learn to live by subtraction.

Society has given you friendship, money, human ties and achievements, and by the time you reach old age you will have acquired a great many things, just like a house that gradually fills up with accumulated objects. If your heart becomes cluttered up with the things you have acquired, then they will end up holding you back.

What do our elderly friends discuss when they get together? A lot of the time, it involves grumbling. They complain that their sons and daughters have no time for them, saying: 'I worked so hard to raise you – I did everything for you – wiped your bottom, changed your nappies! – but now you're busy, no time even for a quick visit.' They grumble at the unfairness of society: 'In my day we were busy making revolution,

Rather than fighting with others, it is better to struggle with yourself, and try to find ways to improve yourself.

and all we got was a few dozen yuan a month – now look at my granddaughter, she went to a foreign company and was earning three or four thousand yuan straight away. Is this fair to people like us who've worked our hearts out?'

If you keep saying things like this, then things that you should find pleasure in will become painful, a hidden burden dragging you down. At this time you need friends to help you come to terms with life, and learn how to let go of things, so that you can leave these annoyances and frustrations far behind you.

One thing we notice from a close reading of the *Analects* is that there are not actually many examples concerned with friendship alone, but that choosing friends is choosing a way of life. The kind of friends we make will first depend on our inner wisdom and self-cultivation; then on our particular circle of friends, and whether these friends are harmful or beneficial to our lives.

In short, once we have focused on our own heart and soul and on those who surround us, we must concern ourselves with what goals we should set ourselves as we move through life.

Part Five

The Way of
Ambition

To be the best person we can be; to have a well-run family, to be of benefit to our country, to bring peace to the world: these are the things we should all aspire to.

When Confucius discussed ambition with his students he did not suggest that the higher your ambition the better. What really matters is that you are firm of purpose and keep true to your inner conviction.

Whether your goals are great or small, the basis for realizing them lies in finding the things that are closest to your heart. Allowing your heart to guide you will always be more important than chasing external achievements.

How should we understand ambition today? Is there a conflict between Confucius's attitudes and our modern goals?

Confucius said: 'The Three Armies can be deprived of their commanding officer, but even a common man cannot be deprived of his purpose.' (*Analects* IX) This is often quoted and it tells us that a person's goals are of the utmost importance, for they determine the development and direction of their whole life.

So when Confucius was teaching, he often made his students talk about their own ambitions. The ninth chapter of *The Analects of Confucius* contains one of the relatively few longer passages, which is called 'Sitting in Attendance', and concerns a free and frank discussion between Confucius and his disciples on the subject of ambition.

One day, Confucius's four disciples Zilu, Zeng Dian, Ran Qiu and Gongxi Chi were sitting with their master. Confucius spoke to them very informally, saying: 'Because I'm a bit older than you, nobody wants to give me an official post. I often hear you say: "Nobody understands my ambition!" Now, suppose there was someone who understood you, and planned to employ you, what would you do?'

Zilu had a hasty character. When he heard his teacher ask this, he instantly replied: 'Give me a middle-sized kingdom with about a thousand war chariots, caught between two larger kingdoms, threatened with invasion from without and food shortages from within. If I am allowed to manage it, in less than three years I will inspire the entire population, and the common people will have come to know the meaning of morality.'

We may feel that Zilu's ambition is pretty impressive, and one might think that a teacher like Confucius, who set so much store by ruling the country through his own principles of ritual and self-cultivation, would have been gratified to see one of his students achieve such a success, and save a nation from peril. Zilu didn't expect that Confucius's reaction would be not merely neutral, but even a little disdainful. 'The Master smiled at him.' He laughed briefly and coldly, without giving a direct response, and then went on to ask the second student: 'Ran Qiu, what is your ambition?'

Ran Qiu's reply was noticeably more modest than Zilu's. He did not dare to mention so large a state, or so many issues. 'If there was a small state of sixty or seventy square leagues, or fifty to sixty square leagues, for me to govern, then after three years, I could give the common people enough food to eat and clothes to wear. As to enlightened government, rites, music and philosophy, that will have to wait on a sage or a *junzi*.' He meant that on a material level he could enrich the common people and give them all they needed, but as for belief in the nation, and bringing prosperity through ritual and music, that's beyond me. Best to wait for a *junzi* who is wiser than me.

When he had finished, his teacher as before gave no direct response. Confucius then proceeded to ask the third student: 'Gongxi Chi! What is your ambition?'

Gongxi Chi was a degree more modest still. He replied: 'I do not say that I already have the ability, but I am ready to learn.' First he stated his own attitude: I make no claims for myself, but since the teacher has asked me this, all I can say is that I am willing to learn. After that he said that he would like to dress in his robes of office and formal cap, to be a minor officiant in the official State rituals, or a minor functionary in meetings with foreign sovereigns and ministers. He did not mention ruling a nation or governing its people at all.

You will have noticed that each of these three students of Confucius was more modest than the last, each was more moderate than the last, each was closer to the starting point of his own life, and further from his ultimate aims.

In today's terms, the most important thing in a person's development is often not how high their ultimate ambition is, but the basis they have right now. We often have no shortage of great plans and aspirations, but we lack a practical road to lead us to our desires, one step at a time.

By this point only one person had not yet spoken, so Confucius asked again: 'Dian, how about you?'

Zeng Dian made no immediate reply. The language used here describes this moment remarkably vividly in just three characters, 鼓瑟希, describing the sound of a burst of music that dies gradually away: up until that point his attention had been completely focused on a lute of fifty strings, which he was playing. When he heard the teacher ask him a question, he let the sound of the lute gradually fade, and then, with a final chord, he brought the melody to a close. Zeng Dian slowly and unhurriedly 'put aside the lute and stood up'. People sat on the ground in those days, and when students were listening to a teacher or holding a discussion, they would kneel, sitting back on their heels, but they had

> We do not lack grand, wide-ranging ambitions, but we lack a proper road to lead us there.

to stand up when replying to the teacher, to show respect. Zeng Dian put the lute aside, and then deferentially got to his feet and answered his teacher.

From these few words of description, we can see that Zeng Dian was a calm and collected type of person; he would not reply in a prompt, impetuous way like Zilu, but instead spoke pleasantly and persuasively, having thought everything through in advance. He first solicited the teacher's opinion, saying: 'My ambition is not the same as my three classmates. Am I allowed to talk about it?' The teacher said: 'What does that matter? I just want every person here to talk about their ambition.'

It was only then that Zeng Dian calmly began. He said: 'My ambition is, at the end of spring, in the third month of the lunar calendar [April or May in the Western calendar], to put on newly made spring clothes, and in the season when all the world is in bloom and all of nature has come back to life, to go with a few adult friends, and a group of children, to bathe together in the waters of the River Yi, now free from the winter's ice. Once we are perfectly clean, we will bask in the spring breeze on the Rain Altar by the side of the River Yi, letting it blow into us and become one with us, to welcome the season of life and vitality along with the heavens and the earth, enjoying a rite of the spirit. When this rite is complete, everybody will happily return home, singing songs. This is all I want.'

When Confucius heard this, he heaved a long sigh and said: 'I am with Dian!' That is to say, Confucius's own ambition was the same as Zeng Dian's. These are the only words of judgement that Confucius uttered throughout the discussion.

When each man had described his ambition, the three students departed. Zeng Dian did not leave at once, but asked his teacher: 'What is your opinion of what those three said?'

At first, Confucius ingeniously deflected the question, replying: 'They were just talking about their own ambitions, that's all.'

But Zeng Dian then asked: 'So why did you laugh when Zilu had finished his speech?'

Once this question had been asked, it was impossible not to reply. Confucius said: 'It is by the rites that a state is administered, but in the way he spoke Zilu showed a lack of modesty. That is why I smiled at him. Courtesy is essential for governing a nation, but Zilu's words were entirely without modesty, so I laughed at him. What he meant was that if you want to govern a nation by means of courtesy and the rites, you must first have kindness, gentleness and a kind of deference, this is the starting point. You saw how hastily Zilu replied, barging in to be first to speak. This shows that he lacked proper deference.'

Following on from this Zeng Dian asked again: 'But didn't Ran Qiu want to govern a nation? So why didn't you laugh at him?'

Confucius said: 'But a state of fifty or sixty square leagues, or less, is still a state, surely?'

Zeng Dian asked again: 'And wasn't Gongxi Chi talking about governing a nation as well? How come you didn't laugh at him?'

Confucius said: 'If you have a temple, and meetings between rulers of the nations, if this isn't governing a country, then what is? If even someone as conversant with the Rites as Gongxi Chi says he wants to be a minor officiant, who is fit to be Master of Ceremonies?'

What Confucius meant was that he did not laugh at Zilu because he thought Zilu lacked the talent to run a state, but for the contents of his speech and his lack of modesty. The issue is not whether the area governed is big or small, or whether or not it is a kingdom; it concerns each student's attitude. Because Ran Qiu's and Gongxi Chi's attitudes were modest, and they had real ability too, Confucius did not laugh at them.

As we have seen, Confucius had no time for those

who make empty boasts. As he said: 'It is rare, indeed, for a man with cunning words and an ingratiating face to be benevolent.' (*Analects* I) He maintained that the true *junzi* should be 'halting in speech but quick in action' (*Analects* IV): superficially, therefore, a *junzi* might not seem to be very impressive, but their inner heart is infinitely strong, resolute and steadfast.

According to an ancient saying there are three things that can never be taken back: a shot arrow, a spoken word and a lost opportunity. Words once spoken are as hard to put back as water spilt from a jug, so a true *junzi* always gets the thing done first, then talks about it.

Confucius said: 'The *junzi* is ashamed of his word outstripping his deed.' (*Analects* XIV) In China we still talk about someone's 'words outstripping his deeds' today. A *junzi* is ashamed for their words to go further than their actions.

A *junzi* does not talk about the things they want to do or the goals they want to achieve; a *junzi* always waits until they have done what they set out to do before casually dropping it into the conversation. This is what is meant by 'he puts his words into action before allowing his words to follow his deeds' (*Analects* II).

There is another question here: since Confucius did not disagree with Zilu, Ran Qiu and Gongxi Chi's ambitions, why did he only give warm encouragement to Zeng Dian? What can we see from Confucius's support of Zeng Dian?

The great Song Dynasty Confucian scholar Zhu Xi has a pretty authoritative reading of this discussion. He said Zeng Dian's ambition amounts to no more than 'Remaining content with the place I am now in, taking joy in its daily business, I have no intention of sacrificing myself for the sake of others.'

Zeng Dian's life consisted of commonplace daily activities and he had no great wish to sacrifice himself for other people but he had a rich and full inner heart. To him, the perfection of his own character was an essential starting point, and his ambition was to see all of nature in its proper place. This means that his professional achievements would also be at a higher level than the other three, whose ambitions were purely professional.

This is what Confucius meant when he said 'the *junzi* is not a vessel'. A true *junzi* never tries to use professional achievements to get a better social position. On the contrary, the *junzi* inevitably sees self-cultivation as a starting point; you must want to begin with the things closest to you, and with perfection of the inner heart.

In Confucius's view, the social responsibility of the *junzi* takes the form of idealism, which is a higher state than professionalism. *Junzi* have never been confined to a particular profession. As he said: 'The *junzi* is no vessel.' (*Analects* II) A vessel in this context means someone who reaches the desired standard and conforms to the rules, doing the job demanded of them, but no more.

We must always remember that human beings are strange creatures; our thoughts determine our actions, which is to say, as we have seen, that our attitude determines everything. The things that each of us do in society every day are generally similar, but we all have a different explanation for them.

> Confucius's strength is forever the strength of action, and not the strength of words.

I once read a book by a fifteenth-century religious reformer, in which he tells a story from when he was young. This story was to change his entire life.

He wrote that one day he walked past a huge building site in the blistering sun, full of men carrying bricks, all streaming with sweat.

He went to ask the first man: 'What are you doing?'

That man said, in a very surly manner: 'Can't you see? It's hard labour – carrying bricks!'

The writer tried his question on a second person. This man's attitude was a lot more placid than the first: he stacked the bricks he was carrying into a neat pile, ran his eyes over them, and then he said: 'I'm building a wall.'

After that he went to ask a third person. There was a sort of cheerful, kindly glow to the man as he put down the bricks he was carrying, raised his head, wiping away the sweat, and said very proudly: 'Are you asking me? We're building a *church*.'

We can see that the things these three people were doing were identical in every way, but their explanations were entirely different.

The first man's attitude I call pessimism. He regarded everything we do as just another burden in a life of toil, focusing on the hardship of the moment (which of course really does exist).

The second man's attitude is what I call professionalism. He knew that he was building a wall, that this wall was part of a completed product, and that he had to do his best and earn his wages. It was his professional duty, and his attitude is well up to standard for professionalism. This is the state that Confucius called 'being a vessel', and as a vessel he was more than adequate. But he did not have any higher calling.

The third kind of attitude I call the idealist attitude. That is to say, he sees every brick in front of him at that moment, and every drop of sweat, and he knows that all this is leading to the creation of a sacred place, a church. He knows that every step he takes is of value, and he knows what the final result of all his hard work will be. At this time, he works as more than just a vessel. The things he does are connected to our life, to our dreams, to whether we can finally build a church. And at the same time, because he is immersed in the dream of a church, he goes beyond individual success to achieve something much greater.

A *junzi*'s role in society adapts to the context, and moves with the times. It is not a *junzi*'s actions that are important, but the motives behind those actions. The *junzi* are the conscience of a society. But being a *junzi* is something that everybody can achieve. That dream, that goal, is both high and far-reaching, but it is not beyond

Every one of us has our own goals, but in the hurried, endlessly repeating cycles and rhythms of work, how much time and space do we have to pay attention to our inner heart? The part of ourselves that performs in a social role is plainly visible, but often we muffle the voice of our own spirit.

our reach, in fact it exists in the here and now, in the inner hearts of each one of us.

I once read a short story about a man who was very unhappy with his life. He suspected it might be the early symptoms of depression, so he went to see a psychiatrist.

He said to the doctor: 'Every day I am terribly afraid of going home from work. When I'm working everything is normal, but as soon as I get back home I feel full of doubts and fears. I don't know what my heart's true ambition is; I don't know what choices I should make. The closer it gets to evening, the worse this feeling of dread becomes, and the pressure gets more and more intense. I often can't sleep a wink all night. But the next day when I go to work in the morning, and enter into my professional role, my symptoms disappear. If this carries on for much longer, I'm afraid I'll go mad.'

When the doctor had heard him out, he made a suggestion: 'There's a famous comedian in our city, he's a fantastic performer, everyone who sees him splits their sides laughing, and forgets all their troubles. To start with, why don't you try going to one of his shows? After that we can have another talk, to see whether it's done anything to help you. Then we'll discuss a plan of action.'

When he had heard this, the man did not speak for a long time. When he finally raised his face to look at the doctor, it was dripping with tears. Almost too overcome to speak, he said: 'I am that comedian.'

This is just a fable, but it is the kind of thing that can very easily happen in our lives today. Think about it: when a person has become accustomed to a role, and cheerfully performs within that role, believing it to be his or her ambition, and a sign of professional success, how much room is left for spiritual longings? How much space have we left outside our roles, for us to truly know our own hearts? This is at the root of the panic and disorientation many people experience when they step outside their professional roles.

> Success in our professional life is not necessarily the heart's true ambition.

There is another interesting little story:

There once were three little field mice running about between the fields, all busy with their preparations to get through the winter.

The field mouse was searching furiously for provisions, carrying all kinds of grain and seeds into his burrow.

The second field mouse was searching for things to keep out the cold, and he dragged a lot of straw and fluffy seed heads into the hole.

And the third field mouse? He kept wandering about

the fields, looking at the sky, then at the earth, and then lying down to rest for a while.

His two hard-working companions rebuked the third mouse as they toiled away, saying: 'You're so lazy, making no preparations to get through the winter, let's see how you manage when winter comes!'

The third field mouse made no attempt to explain himself.

Things that on the surface appear to be completely valueless, can in fact be a starting point for us to bring calm and stability to the inner heart.

Later, when winter arrived, the three field mice hid themselves away in a cramped little burrow. They had no shortage of food and had everything they needed to keep out the cold, but they had nothing to get on with all day. Gradually, boredom set in, and they had no idea how to pass the time.

So the third field mouse started to tell stories to the other two: about how he met a child on the edge of the field one autumn afternoon, and what he saw the child doing; about a man he saw by the pond one autumn morning, and what he was doing. He told them about conversations he had had; and a song he had heard from a bird . . .

It was only then that his two companions realized that this field mouse had been collecting sunshine to get them through the winter.

If we look again at Zeng Dian's ambition now: to hold a rite to cleanse himself and get close to nature, in the season when the earth has thrown off the shackles of winter and all of nature is rejoicing. While it appears to have no practical significance whatever, such rituals can bring peace and order to the inner heart. To enjoy such peace and order, we must be as one with the heavens and the earth, able to keenly perceive the changes in nature's rhythms, and to experience the four seasons, and the natural landscape of mountains and rivers, the wind and the moon.

To us today, this is a great luxury. In our modern world, there are too many things that are out of season: in the heat of summer, our homes have air conditioning to waft us with cool breezes; when the cold winter comes, central heating makes the house as warm as spring; at Chinese New Year at the end of winter, the table is loaded with brightly coloured vegetables, grown in polytunnels. When life grows oversimplified like this, the traces left in our lives by the four passing seasons become blurred; seasonal changes and the annual patterns of nature can no longer arouse any reaction in our hearts. We lack Zeng Dian's sensitivity – sensitivity that made him wish, at the height of spring, to let himself be shaped by it – and thereby lack this platform from which we can let our larger ambitions take wing and fly.

The relationship between our goals and our actions is just like that of a kite and a string. The key to how far a kite can fly is in the string in your hands. And this string is the aspirations of your inner heart. The more calm, matter-of-fact and steady your mind, the easier you will find it to reject grandiose, showy external things, and respectfully listen to the tranquil voice of your inner heart. This means that when you take up a role in society, you will not lose touch with yourself; you will be able to bear your responsibilities cheerfully, and to achieve the very best.

Many people feel that the ambitions described in 'Sitting in Attendance' differ somewhat from our usual understanding of what Confucius and his students had to say on the subject of ambition. For example, contrary to what Zengzi says at another point, these ambitions are not heavy: 'A Gentleman must be strong and resolute, for his burden is heavy and the road is long.' (*Analects* VIII)

But if we stop and think about it for a moment, the attitudes described in 'Sitting in Attendance' are in fact the trees on which those 'burdens', those great personal and social ambitions, will grow and bear fruit. If, in their professional role, a person lacks this sense of calm, or an understanding of his or her inner heart, they will only be good for giving orders, and have no hope of improving themselves.

The key to remember is that this self-improvement is not selfish. Confucius's emphasis on the cultivation of our inner heart in no way suggests that we should relinquish our responsibility to society; rather, we cultivate ourselves so that we can better serve society.

In China, there is a type of person, the *shi*, who are the highest intellectual class, people who see the society in which they live as their own responsibility. It is a very honourable status sometimes referred to as that of a 'gentleman-scholar'.

Confucius once said: 'A *shi* who is attached to a settled home is not worthy of being a shi.' (*Analects* XIV) In other words, if someone spends their days with no room in their head for anything but their own small family circle, and their own mundane, day-to-day affairs, then they cannot become a true *shi*.

It is just this aspect of responsibility that Confucius's student Zigong touches upon when he asks Confucius: 'What must a man be like before he can be said truly to be a *shi*?'

His teacher told him: 'A man who can control himself and who, when sent abroad, does not disgrace the commission of his lord can be said to be a *shi*.'

What Confucius meant was that people must understand courtesy and integrity, they must be to be able to control their behaviour; they must have a firm, steadfast heart and will not compromise their standards; while at the same time they must be useful to society – that is, they must work for the good of society. In other words, once a person has achieved this inner cultivation, they will not allow themselves to become complacent; they will continue to go out and do useful things; they will be loyal to their mission, and 'not disgrace the commission of their lord'. This is, according to Confucius, the highest standard for the *shi*. And it is not easy, because there is no way of knowing in advance what your mission might be.

Zigong thought this standard was too high, so he asked: 'May I ask about the grade below?' Is there another standard that's a bit lower?

Confucius replied: 'Someone praised for being a good son in his clan and for being a respectful young man in the village.' In other words, someone praised by their extended family for being good to their parents, and popular in their village for the respectful behaviour shown towards fellow villagers. If you can start from what is around you, if you can shine with the light of human love and human ties and use the strength of this love to win the approval of those around you, and not shame your ancestors, this is the second level of *shi*.

Zigong asked again: 'And the next?' Is there another, lower level?

Confucius said: 'A man who insists on keeping his word and seeing his actions through to the end could, perhaps, come next, even though he sometimes shows a stubborn petty-mindedness.'

Modern readers will probably be flabbergasted by this. Such high standards of behaviour only let you into the third class of *shi*? A person who insists on keeping his or her word and seeing their actions through to the end, who, having once agreed to do something, will get it done, regardless of the methods used, and regardless of the consequences, who always keeps their promises – all this, and this person can only at a pinch be classed as a third-class *shi*? How many people today can actually manage to insist on keeping their word and seeing their actions through to the end?

Although they are difficult to achieve, these three

> The Master said: 'There is no point in seeking the views of the *shi* who, though he sets his heart on the Way, is ashamed of poor food and poor clothes.' (*Analects* IV)

standards are, according to Confucius, what define the sort of mature individual who can successfully take on any position in society.

There is a story about Lin Xiangru, the famous minister of the kingdom of Zhao during the Period of the Warring States (475–221 BC); which helps to demonstrate the highest standard of *shi*: the person who 'does not disgrace the commission of his lord'.

It happened that the King of Zhao acquired the Hesheng Jade, a jewel of incalculable rarity and value, worth more than many cities. The King of Qin was eager to get his hands on it, so he sent an ambassador to the King of Zhao, saying that he was prepared to exchange fifteen of his cities for this piece of jade. The King of Zhao knew that Qin was a ruthless and greedy kingdom: once the piece of jade reached Qin it would be impossible to get it back. But Lin Xiangru said: 'If we don't take the Jade, we will put ourselves in the wrong. I'll take the jewel and if I can't get the fifteen cities that were promised, I will lay down my life rather than let it fall into the hands of the King of Qin. So, as long as you have me, you have the Jade.'

When Lin Xiangru arrived in the Kingdom of Qin bearing the Hesheng Jade, the King of Qin received him casually in a side hall, and allowed his ministers and the ladies of the court to pass the priceless treasure around, sniggering amongst themselves. When Lin Xiangru saw this, he realized that the Kingdom of Zhao was being treated with the same lack of respect as the Jade. However, getting the jewel back would be no easy task. So he said to the King of Qin: 'Your Majesty, this jade has a flaw, give it to me and I will show you.' When the King of Qin returned that piece of jade into his hands, Lin Xiangru retreated several paces, backing up against a pillar. He stood there and clutched the stone and, in a towering rage, he said to the King of Qin: 'When you received our treasure in such a place as this, you dishonoured both this Jade, and the Kingdom of Zhao. Before we came, we burned incense, made sacrifices and fasted for fifteen days, as a mark of respect to the Kingdom of Qin. I came here reverently bearing the Jade, but you casually handed it over to your ministers and court beauties. I can see from your cavalier attitude that you have no real intention of giving us fifteen cities in exchange. If you really want it, you should fast and burn incense for fifteen days as we did, and hand over those fifteen cities and then I will return the Jade to you. If you don't do this, I will shatter both my head and this piece of jade at the same instant on the great pillar of your Golden Hall.' The King of Qin was afraid, and hurriedly agreed to his demands.

Lin Xiangru knew that the King of Qin would not keep his word, and so he ordered his family to flee overnight back to Zhao, taking the treasure with them. He, however, remained behind, and confessed what he had done to the King of Qin. He said: 'I know that you have no real intention of giving us those cities, but by now the Jade has already returned intact to Zhao.'

Stories of this kind are not uncommon in the ancient books and records of classical China. The way in which someone approaches a professional task when everything around them suddenly changes is a good test of that person's maturity. How can a person conquer their fear; how can they remain calm, collected and unflustered? For this, we need to find something on which we can rest our hopes. It may not necessarily be something commonly viewed as a great ambition: power, money or anything of that sort. It could be said that each of us in the great circle of life has one goal that they care about more than anything else. And anyone who can find such an ideal on which to pin their hopes will have an anchor for their whole life and a firm foundation for their inner heart.

For Confucius, all great goals are built upon such plain and simple foundations. Positive thinking is one of the most powerful forces in the world and what we all crave is time for reflection – not material luxury, but the luxury of a spiritual journey.

Confucius once said that he wanted to go to live in the remote eastern region of China populated by non-Han Chinese, and known at that time as the land of the Nine Barbarian Tribes.

Somebody tried to talk him out of it, saying: 'But could you put up with their uncouth ways?' Could you stand to live in such a poor, backward place?

Confucius replied simply, 'Once a *junzi* settles amongst them, what uncouthness will there be?'

There are two interpretations of his reply. The first is that the *junzi*'s 'mission' is to the whole world; to the *junzi* a place is no more than an external environment, whether it is rich and luxurious, or simple and crude. Secondly, the mind of a *junzi* has a constant, stable energy, which can make the things around them light up and burst into flower. The atmosphere they create around themselves and within their own life can transform even a backward, uncouth place.

In China we have a very well-known poem written in the Tang Dynasty called 'On My Humble House', by Liu Yuxi, in which he demonstrates the response of all China's gentleman-scholars throughout the ages to life in humble surroundings. He said that we might not be able to change the material environment we live in, but there is no need to be too exacting in our demands, for it is the people around us who create our most important environment.

He spoke of 'the laughter of the cultured and wise', describing how 'no vulgarity may enter in'. In other words, a person's home may be poor and ramshackle, but it is the place in which they and their friends discuss their dreams and ambitions. and therefore their humble living conditions are not what really matters.

> The Way of ambition will give us a fixed, accessible starting point, and a resource and storehouse of inner happiness.

How, then, should we reach our goal? We should take a simple, commonplace starting point, which will lead us to spiritual happiness.

When we really understand 'Sitting in Attendance'; when we have read those heartfelt words 'I am with Dian'; when we know that such a sage, an example for all of us throughout the ages, wished for a life of 'bathing in the River Yi, and enjoying the breeze on the Rain Altar', and wanted in the late spring to 'go home chanting poetry', we will see that his desire is in fact very similar to that solitary communion with the spirits of heaven and earth described by the philosopher Zhuangzi.

In other words, the ancient sages and men of virtue all started out on their spiritual journey from a fixed core:

their own personal values. First they came to understand the yearnings of their own spirit, and only then could they make great plans or form grand ambitions.

We all want to find the fixed points in our lives, so that we too can find a starting point for the long journey ahead of us. Let us build a wisdom of the soul, founded on the wisdom that comes from self-knowledge; let us enter into the wisdom of Confucius, so that we too can be his peaceful students, overcoming the changes and turmoil of the ages to see his serene, steady, peaceful face today. Let us remember his encouragement to get close to nature, and, in the rare intervals in our crowded, busy lives, treat ourselves to a small, private rite of the soul, unlike that comedian whose personality was split, and who no longer dared to face his inner heart. In fact, in our modern era, the serenity we find in Confucius's everyday concepts, the clarity and truth of his ideas, and the strength we find within them should encourage us to cherish our inner hearts, and recognize that the roots of all of our ambitions and goals are found deep within us.

Confucius never forgot how difficult this was. But his teachings guide us through the different challenges we face as we grow older. He helps us understand what is required of us at every stage on our journey through life.

Part Six

The Way of
Being

Confucius described his life as having six stages.

His description of his journey through life still has a great deal of significance for us in the modern world today.

The key is recognizing what he wants us to draw from this wisdom, to make our lives more effective and of greater value.

Throughout history, people have lamented the passing of time more than anything else.

Everyone in China also knows the couplet written by Sun Ran for the twin pillars of the Daguan Pavilion in Kunming. The first line says: 'The five hundred *li* of Lake Dianchi spread out before your eyes.' The second goes 'Thousands of years of things past come at once to mind.'

To a philosopher, the surging, flowing waters of a river are not only a natural phenomenon. Another thing that flows away like the waters of a river and can never be held back or returned to the way it was is time.

In his poem 'Lament by the River' the poet Du Fu wrote: 'I weep for my past life, and tears soak my garments. The river waters roll by, unchanging and without end.' And in 'Contemplating the Past on Mount Xisai' Liu Yuxi said: 'In our human life, how many sources there are of grief and regret! The mountains stand unchanging, as the cold winter river flows between them.' Human life is but a short span, while nature is eternal; the powerful contrast is enough to jolt the spirit and bring tears of sorrow to our eyes.

It is no wonder that that Tang Dynasty poet Zhang Ruoxu posed this eternal question to the moon in 'Moonlight Night on the River':

Who was the first man to see the moon on the river bank? In what year did the moon first shine on man? Human lives ceaselessly come and go, generation after generation, but the river and the moon remain constant year after year. I don't know who the river and the moon are waiting for, I only see the waters of the Yangtze flowing away.

Confucius was no exception. 'While standing by a river, Confucius said: "What passes away is, perhaps, like this."' Everybody in China knows these words. It is an obscure phrase, only just hinting at its meaning, but it carries within it a deep regret at the changes and hardships of human life.

In the midst of this vast, endless universe, amid the unending cycles of nature, each human life is so tiny and insignificant, passing in the blink of an eye. So how should we plan our brief lives?

At the same time that Confucius was sighing over the water as it flowed past, he described a path through life to his students, and to thousands of generations after them:

At fifteen I set my heart on learning; at thirty I took my stand; at forty I came to be free from doubts; at fifty I understood the Decree of Heaven; at sixty my ear was attuned; at seventy I followed my heart's desire without overstepping the line. (Analects II)

This is a rough set of coordinates for human life, in which several stages are particularly emphasized. Let's take a quick look at the path through life that the Sage describes for us, to see what lessons we can draw from it, and what it means to us today.

A human life is no more than a brief moment borrowed from time; as the months and years flow past, we take these few brief years and carve them into a certain shape, hoping to create something eternal, to be our memorial once we are gone.

As we have seen, we all have ambitions and things that motivate us, but we have to begin by coming to terms with the society we live in. Study begins with the transformation of a natural, unformed human being into a person shaped by the rules of society. When Confucius says 'At fifteen I set my heart on learning', he is describing his own starting point on that journey, and it was also what he required of his students.

Confucius himself often said: 'I was not born with knowledge but, being fond of antiquity, I am quick to seek it.' (*Analects* VII) Even Confucius was not born understanding everything. But because he was deeply interested in the culture and the experiences of the ancients, he was able to work tirelessly and study diligently.

Today we want to build a society where education is freely available to all. But what kind of learning is good learning?

In today's age of information there are just too many things to learn. Today's children no longer wait until fifteen to 'set the heart on learning'; many start learning before they are even five years old. But what do they actually learn? A few children memorize the values of π to many places after the decimal point; others can recite long poems in classical Chinese as a party piece for guests. But will these things really be useful for the rest of their lives? How many of today's 'inclinations to learning' are what Confucius spoke of as 'studying in order to improve oneself'? And how many are studying in order to make use of what they have learned?

In the modern age, the most distressing thing for us is that there is too much information; our biggest difficulty is that of choice. We desperately need a well-laid-out plan to guide us through the maze of choice so that we can learn what we really need to learn.

Confucius's attitude was always that going to 'excess is worse than not far enough'. The best things all have degree; if you are greedy you will bite off more than you can chew, and your brain will become like the hard drive of a computer, full of passive knowledge that is not doing anything. You would do better to make use of your limited knowledge and study in order to master just one subject, to absorb it into your life.

Confucius said: 'If one learns from others but does not think, one will be bewildered. If, on the other hand, one thinks but does not learn from others, one will be in peril.' (*Analects* II) We must learn, think and make use of what we have learned, all at the same time.

In China our present college education system hands out knowledge in standardized lengths, but we can add more breadth to it. Confucius's preferred method of learning, in which thinking and learning are combined, has a lot to teach us.

Through study, experience and training, we will gradually advance, coming to understand things both

> 'At thirty I took my stand.'
>
> In China, 'taking one's stand at thirty' is still a phrase that you will very often hear. At this age, just about everybody begins to look inside themselves, asking: 'Have I taken my stand?'
>
> So what is taking one's stand? Do you have to have a car, a flat, or some professional position before you can be said to have taken your stand? And how does reaching the age of thirty, which in China we call the year of taking a stand, affect us?

intellectually and intuitively. This will be the state we are in as thirty approaches.

These days, we seem to reach adulthood later and later, especially in the big cities, where thirty-year-olds still get called 'boys' and 'girls'. So how are we to judge whether a person has 'taken their stand' in the world? And what responsibilities does taking a stand entail?

For example, when children have just started at primary school, they believe that the sun is bright, flowers are a beautiful bright red, people's hearts are good, that the world is full of tender feelings, that the prince and the princess will come together in the end, and that there is no sorrow or distress in life.

But once they reach their teenage years, a powerful tendency to rebel will emerge, and in their twenties, when they have just entered adult society, they will feel that nothing in the world is the way it should be, that the adult world has cheated them, that life is full of ugliness, wretchedness and deceit. These are the 'angry young men' that we often hear about. This part of growing up has its own special bleakness, which is an inevitable reaction to the first stage. But by the time we hit thirty, we should be at the stage of fulfilment, which means neither thinking that everything in front of you is bright and sunny, as a ten-year-old would, nor that everything is bleak and cruel, like people in their twenties.

> 'Taking a stand at thirty' is building up inner confidence.

Taking a stand at thirty is first and foremost an inner stand; finding your place within society comes afterwards.

From the point of view of inner spiritual independence, truly good learning means applying all that we have learned to ourselves, so that the things we have learned become our own. This is the kind of study that China's culture demands of us.

So the period from fifteen to thirty is about the process of learning. But how is one to arrive at this integrated state, where all that we have learned becomes our own?

Chinese people traditionally approach learning in two ways: one we call 'I explain the Six Classics', the other 'the Six Classics explain me'.

The first method requires a lifelong study of the classics, lasting well into old age; by the time your hair is white and you have finished reading all the books, you will be fit to make commentaries on the classics.

But the second method, 'the Six Classics explain me', is on an altogether higher plane. It involves using the spirit of the Classics to explain and inform your own life.

Thirty is the age at which to build up inner self-confidence. This self-confidence is not set up in opposition to external things. Rather it creates a kind of harmony, in which both internal and external are lifted up. This is like the couplet on Mount Tai: 'The sea reaches out to its furthest extreme, the sky is a shore: On ascending the summit, I will be another peak of the mountain.' This is one of the ways in which the Chinese relate to mountains and rivers. Our aim is not to conquer or subjugate them, instead, the mountains and rivers are seen as elevating us. Just as the sea stretches away endlessly, with no shore but the sky, making it seem as if the whole world is stretched out before us, on reaching the topmost pinnacle of a mountain, it is not so much that I am trampling the high mountain beneath my feet, but that the mountain peak on which I stand has raised me to new heights.

This is the state that we call 'the Six Classics explain me'.

Confucius always taught his students to live plainly and simply: do what is in front of you as well as you can; there's no need to worry about most things, so don't worry about them.

For example, it is well known that 'The topics Confucius did not speak of were prodigies, force, disorder and gods.' (*Analects* VII) Confucius did not like to talk about things like gods and spirits, because his attention was focused on real, tangible behaviour.

When Zilu asked him once about ghosts and spirits, Confucius said calmly: 'You are not able even to serve man. How can you serve the spirits?' You can't even get living people's business straight in your head; how can you think of going to honour dead people? That is to say, before you start to study you should keep things simple, beginning with what is in front of you. Don't immediately go pondering empty, profound things.

Zilu was not ready to give up, and said: 'May I ask about death?'

Again, Confucius said serenely: 'You do not even understand life. How can you understand death?'

This still has such a lot to teach us today. When studying, first do your very best to understand the things in life that are within your reach. Do not overstretch yourself to ponder things that are beyond you or deeply profound. Until we reach the age of taking one's stand, it is only through learning a little bit at a time that we can truly stand up.

For me, then, 'taking one's stand at thirty' is not a means of evaluating whether or not you have measured up to any external social standards. But rather it is a way of evaluating your life against internal standards, of the heart and the soul, in order to establish whether you have begun to acquire bright, calm, unhurried introspection, and therefore whether you have reached a state where you can deal confidently and decisively with your own affairs.

Going beyond material gain and focusing on what is within, is, for me, the greatest proof that one has taken one's stand.

There are many examples of this attitude in Chinese culture. Take the old man in the straw rain hat in Liu Zongyuan's poem, 'fishing alone in the snowy winter river' in the bitter cold of winter, dangling his hook for nothing but its own sake. Or take the great poet and scholar Wang Huizhi's journey in a small boat on a snowy night to visit his friend Dai Kui: when he came to his friend's door he turned and left without bothering to knock. Why? Because he had come on an impulse, missing his friend; when he reached his friend's door the impulse vanished, and he went home. These ancients were loyal to their own souls; the direction shown to them by their heart determined the direction of their actions.

Between thirty and forty, people move on from the years of 'taking one's stand' to what Confucius called the years of 'freedom from doubts'.

These should be the best years of our lives.

But can everybody achieve 'freedom from doubts' by the age of forty?

In our modern society, people in their forties have reached the middle years of life. They are known and respected in their chosen profession, but they have an older generation above them, a younger generation below, and this puts great pressure on them. In such a testing situation, what is the best way to keep our hearts free from doubts and anxiety?

Confucius frequently elaborates on the idea of 'freedom from doubts'. How can a person truly achieve freedom from doubts and fears? It requires great wisdom.

The years from taking one's stand to freedom from doubts are the best time of our life. Before the age of thirty, people live by addition, constantly acquiring the things they need from the world: experience, wealth, relationships, reputation, and so on. But the more material things we have, the more perplexed and doubtful we become.

After thirty, we have to start learning to live by subtraction – you must learn to let go of the things that are not what your soul really needs.

Our heart is like a new house: when its owners have just moved in, they want to fill it up with furniture, curtains and other decorations. As a result, the house ends up as cluttered as a narrow Beijing alley, full of odds and ends, and we have nowhere left to put ourselves. We become enslaved by our possessions.

Learning to live by subtraction means shedding the people we do not want to be our friends, refusing to do the things we do not want to do, and turning down the money that we do not want to earn. Only when we dare to let go, and know how to let go, can we truly free ourselves from doubts.

So what is freedom from doubts? It is when a person can think and act according to the ideas explored in the 'Doctrine of the Mean'

The Doctrine of the Mean is one of the Four Books that became the core texts of Confucian learning, and which helped define the highest standards of behaviour in ancient China. Philosophically speaking, it concerns the most appropriate 'degree' to which a thing is done. Often nowadays it is mistakenly understood to imply mediocrity, slyness and low cunning; *The Doctrine of the Mean* is widely seen as representing compromise at the expense of principle, perhaps even a blurring of the line between right and wrong.

The Doctrine of the Mean says: 'When happiness, anger, grief and joy are not expressed, this is called the Mean; when they do find expression, but in a restrained and balanced way, this is called Harmony. The Mean is the great root of the world, Harmony is the great Way of the world.' That is to say, the ideal state is one where everything is in harmony, with heaven, earth and all of nature each safely in its own place. This attitude means that even if the outside world treats you unfairly, you now know where you stand and knowing this will help you to cope with the blows and regrets that life metes out and will give you a foothold in life.

When it comes to judging the best ways of doing things, if one does not care which method is correct, and concentrates only on which method is most appropriate, the most appropriate way almost never involves going to extremes.

The great philosopher Feng Youlan once said: 'Learn from the dynasties of old to help the new order; our ideals should be the very highest, but our actions should follow the Way of the Mean.' The Way of the Mean actually entails reaching a very high moral state by the most appropriate method. As the Chinese ancients said: 'At their extremes, glory and radiance return to the Middle Way.' In your twenties and thirties you forge your way ahead through life, but it is not until you have reached forty, the years of freedom from doubts, that you can show tranquil level-headedness and a sense of responsibility. And when someone has reached this stage, a change will take place in many of that person's standards.

Then, when another ten years have passed, and we reach fifty, more changes will have taken place.

*

At fifty, Confucius said that he 'understood the Will of Heaven'. What did he mean? Is it what we mean when we say: 'If a thing is fated it will happen sooner or later, if a thing is not fated to be, don't try to force it'? Does it mean that when we reach fifty we must resign ourselves to our fate?

If we want to answer this question, we must first of all be clear on what exactly Confucius means by understanding the will of Heaven.

Confucius said: 'I do not blame Heaven, nor do I blame Man. In my studies, I start from below and get through to what is up above. If I am understood at all, it is perhaps by Heaven.' (*Analects* XIV) The classical scholar of linguistics, Huang Kan interprets this as: 'Starting from below is studying the affairs of man; getting through to what is above is reaching the will of Heaven. I have made a study of the affairs of man: the affairs of man have good luck and bad, therefore I do not blame Man; above is the will of Heaven, the will of

The more material things they have, the easier it becomes for people to get confused.

Heaven can be for you or against you, therefore I do not blame Heaven.' As we can see, the key to this is the word 'understand': you must be able to come to terms with whatever fate has in store for you. When you can do this, whether it is favourable or unfavourable, know all the good and bad in our world, and know that all of this is in fact all very natural, then you can tackle it rationally and respond to it calmly.

'I do not blame Heaven, I do not blame Man' might be words that are often said, even today, but they are much easier said than done. If you can stop yourself complaining, if you can keep all your carping and criticism bound firmly in your heart, then you will become the sort of person who no longer shunts blame on to others.

This idea of keeping quiet also relates to speaking ill of others. Confucius said: 'The *junzi* gets through to what is above; the petty gets through to what is down below.' (*Analects* XIV) Only the petty spend all their time in malicious gossip and personal disputes. The *junzi*, on the other hand, pays more attention to the inner heart, building a set of convictions for themselves and pursuing their destiny. Confucius said: 'A man has no way of becoming a *junzi* unless he understands Destiny; he has no way of taking his stand unless he understands the rites; he has no way of judging men unless he understands words.' (*Analects* xx)

He believed that the perfection of a person's inner heart and their desire to conform to their destiny were so much more important than imposing their demands on society or making people behave in a particular way.

For Confucius, the three stages of life – 'understanding destiny', 'understanding the rites of society' and 'understanding words' – occur in reverse order. First, we learn words and we come to understand other people and the society we live in through talking to one another and reading books; but understanding words alone is not enough for you to find your feet in society. But we also need to understand ceremony and ritual, all of the things that enable you to respect others. A little more respect will leave you with fewer complaints. The highest level is understanding destiny. To understand destiny is to become a *junzi*, Confucius's ideal, at which point we will have created a self-contained system of values for ourselves, our inner heart will be suffused with a calm, matter-of-fact strength, and we can use this strength in all our interactions with the external world.

Knowing the will of Heaven means that, at fifty you will have an inner firmness of purpose. You will have achieved the state of 'not blaming Heaven and not blaming Man': you will remain unswayed by external things.

The ancient philosopher Zhuangzi has a very similar outlook: 'When all the world flattered him it did not make him increase his efforts, when the whole world condemned him it did not make him downhearted. He drew a clear line between what was inside and what was outside, and understood the difference between true glory and disgrace, but he stopped here.'

In other words, when all the world is praising you, you will not react to this praise and, equally, when all around you are finding fault with you and saying that you have done wrong, you will not lose heart, but will persist, unwavering, in the beliefs you have fixed upon. This is what is meant by 'drawing a clear line between what is inside and what is outside', and understanding 'glory' and 'disgrace'.

What we call growing and maturing is a process by which the inner heart gradually becomes stronger through experience, and we acquire the ability to take external things and transform them into inner strength.

The state of 'understanding the will of heaven' is something we in China tend to naturally associate with the kung-fu novels of Jin Yong.

In Chinese martial arts novels, when a young swordsman first appears on the scene, he generally wields a precious sword of incomparable sharpness, without equal throughout the land, and makes a splendid show with his whistling blade and balletic, graceful bearing. But by the time he has improved his martial skills through dedication and practice, has truly settled down to the life of a swordsman, and become a fighter of some little fame, the sword he uses may just be a blunt blade which he has never bothered to sharpen. By this stage, however, sharpness no longer matters to him, as his inner wisdom and experience have become richer and more solid. And by the time this man has become a famous master swordsman, and his skills have overcome all the champions the other schools had sent to defeat him, he may have no sword at all, just a stick. To him, the sharpness and quality of the metal are no longer important; anything he cares to pick up will do. By the time he has attained the highest state of all – the state of Dugu Qiubai, the hero who sought endlessly for an opponent who could match him in battle – he carries no weapon at all: all his martial arts skills have been subsumed into his heart and mind through years of deep study, and he can create the essence of a sword by just

> Knowing the will of Heaven is a kind of fixity of purpose, and we can use this fixity of purpose to deal with the outside world.

stretching out his hands. By this time his enemies have no strategies or tricks to match him, because he has already reached the state where he needs none. Since he fights without strategies or tricks, his opponent is left baffled, unable to work out what he has done, and powerless to defeat him

In Chinese culture the highest state that any person can reach is that of mastery. What Confucius called 'knowing the will of Heaven' is achieved through years of deep study and practice, absorbing all kinds of truths and through them finally achieving harmony and self-

Confucius said: 'At sixty my ear was attuned'. But what does this mean? As we will see, an 'attuned ear' is the ability to listen to any words, no matter what kind of words they are, and when looking at any issue, to always take the point of view of the person who spoke the words.

However, in real life, we often meet with things that don't go the way we would wish, and hear things that are not pleasant to hear. How can we really achieve an attuned ear?

elevation. And only then will you be ready to reach the next state.

Once you have a thorough understanding of the will of Heaven, and a great inner strength of purpose, you will reach the state that Confucius described as having an attuned ear. You will have attained the greatest possible ability to respect others, you can understand the argument behind any issue, you can listen to all kinds of voices with an open mind, and put yourself in other people's shoes, to understand why they say the things they do.

Attuning the ear is a sympathy for the world and all the people in it, that is, understanding and tolerance.

There is a common Chinese expression which describes this and it roughly translates as 'grieve for the world and pity the people'. In other words, by knowing everyone's motives and desires, you will achieve greater understanding and tolerance.

When we see other people's ways of life through our own value system, we may be shocked; but if we know what brought that person to the place where they are today, then perhaps we can be a bit more understanding.

There is an old saying: Two clouds can only come together to produce rain when they meet at the same height.

So who are the people who have attuned their ears? They are those who, whether their cloud is five thousand or five hundred metres high, are always aware of where the other person's is. This is the way in which Confucius dealt with all his different students, fitting each lesson to suit the pupil.

Those who want to achieve an attuned ear must make themselves infinitely open and expansive; be able to meet with minds at many different heights; not stick to their own unvarying standards and stubbornly remain at the same height, like the man in the folk story who dropped his sword from his boat and made a notch on the side so he could fish the sword out once he got to the shore, or the man in another folk story who, having once managed to catch a rabbit that ran into a tree and stunned itself, spent days sitting by the same tree, waiting for another rabbit to come along.

After taking in all knowledge, and being forged in the refiner's fire, all our study and hard work will bring us to a genuine mastery of our knowledge.

It's just like a common school physics experiment, where the teacher hands out a pencil and a circle divided into seven parts, which are coloured in with the seven colours of the rainbow, then pierced with the pencil and spun round at speed to reveal the colour white. A colour

> Confucius said: 'At seventy I followed my heart's desire
> without overstepping the line.' What does this mean?
> When all rules and high principles have become habits of
> life, you will be able to successfully follow your heart's
> desire. This is the highest state that any individual can
> aim at. But although such a state as this seems to be easy
> and accessible, a person must first be tempered by a
> thousand blows of the hammer before he or she can
> reach this state.

that is created by the blending of the seven vivid colours of the rainbow.

Confucius's state of 'the attuned ear' is the fusion of the rules of the external world within our inner heart. Only once you have this coming together as a foundation for all the rest, can you reach the highest Confucian state.

I once read the following story:

There was once an image of the Buddha in a temple. This statue was exquisitely carved from granite, and every day many people came to pray in front of it. The steps leading up to this Buddha were cut from the same granite from which the statue had been taken.

Finally one day these steps became discontented and raised a protest, saying: 'We started out as brothers, we both came from the body of the same mountain. What gives them the right to trample on us but bow down to you? What's so great about you?'

The Buddha statue said calmly to them: 'That's because it only took four blows of the knife to make you what you are today, but I had to suffer ten thousand cuts and blows before I could become a Buddha.'

Looking at the state of human life that Confucius described, the further through life we get the more he emphasizes the inner heart, and the more calm and relaxed we should become, but before you can reach this state of calm, you must be forged and remade hundreds and thousands of times.

We should view the progression of human life from fifteen to seventy that Confucius described as like a mirror held up to us, in which we can examine ourselves at different stages in our lives. Through it, we will be able to see whether our own spirit has taken its stand, whether we have started to lose some of our doubts, whether we are starting to take in the great truths of the world, whether we can show understanding and compassion towards others' failings, and whether we have managed to follow our heart's desire. If, at twenty or thirty, we can reach, ahead of schedule, the state we should be in at forty and fifty and have already built up a clear and lucid system of values, and are already able to transform the pressures of our society into a flexible strength that will allow us to bounce back, and if we are able to achieve a kind of calm, steady pursuit of our heart's desire without overstepping the line . . . then we can safely say that we have lived a truly meaningful life.

Scientists once performed the following experiment:

In order to obtain an exact measurement of endurance of the common pumpkin, they placed weights on a group of pumpkins, at the very limit of what each could bear.

All the different pumpkins were supporting different weights, but one particular pumpkin was under the most pressure. From a few grams one day to tens of grams the next, to hundreds of grams, and finally to kilograms, by the time this pumpkin had matured, it had a weight of several hundred kilograms pressing down on it.

At the end of the experiment the scientists cut open the pumpkin and its fellows, to see if there was anything unusual about them.

Other pumpkins opened easily at the first blow of the knife, but knives bounced right off this pumpkin, and in the end they had to hack it open using a chainsaw. Its flesh was as tough as the wood of a mature tree!

What experiment is this? It is an experiment of life, a portrait of us all in the modern environment in which we live, and of the flexible strength of our hearts.

Faced with competition and pressure like today's, what reason do we have not to become mature ahead of time? The words of Chairman Mao's poem: 'Seize every moment, for ten thousand years are too long' could not be more appropriate today. If ten thousand years are too long, so too are seventy.

The study of *The Analects of Confucius*, of any of the great classics, and of all the experiences of the ancient sages and wise men, ultimately has only one, essential purpose: to make our lives more meaningful under the radiance of their wisdom, to shorten the road we have to travel, to make us start to feel and think as early as possible like a *junzi*, full of benevolence and kindness, to be able to live up to the *junzi*'s standards of social justice, and to be able to stand up with pride and give a good account of our inner hearts and our professional and social duties.

Only by building up a system of values for the heart, can we change pressure into flexibility and spring back.

I believe that the most important thing about the sages is the way in which they describe the great journey of human life in simple language, and the way their children, grandchildren and remote descendants put it into practice, generation after generation, whether in ignorance or with intent, painfully or joyfully. In this way, the soul of a nation was formed.

Wherever we are, we can let the spiritual power of the ancient classics combine with our contemporary laws and rules, fusing seamlessly together to become an essential component of our lives, to let every one of us build for ourselves a truly worthwhile life. This is surely the ultimate significance of Confucius in our lives today.

First published 2006 by Zhonghua Book Company

First published in Great Britain 2009 by Macmillan
an imprint of Pan Macmillan Ltd
Pan Macmillan, 20 New Wharf Road, London N1 9RR
Basingstoke and Oxford
Associated companies throughout the world
www.panmacmillan.com

ISBN 978-0-330-46453-6

A CIP catalogue record for this book is available from
the British Library.

Printed in the UK by Butler Tanner & Dennis, Frome, Somerset

Visit www.panmacmillan.com to read more about all our books
and to buy them. You will also find features, author interviews and
news of any author events, and you can sign up for e-newsletters
so that you're always first to hear about our new releases.

SUMMON'S MISCELLANY OF SAINTS AND SINNERS

Parminder Summon

CANTERBURY
PRESS

Norwich

First published in 2005 by the Canterbury Press Norwich
(a publishing imprint of Hymns Ancient & Modern
Limited, a registered charity)
9–17 St Albans Place, London N1 0NX

www.scm-canterburypress.co.uk

British Library Cataloguing in Publication data

A catalogue record for this book is available
from the British Library

ISBN 1-85311-667-X/9781-85311-667-4

Typeset by Regent Typesetting, London
Printed and bound by
Creative Print and Design, Wales

For Neville and Kate

In appreciation of your friendship

CONTENTS

INTRODUCTION

Saint: *A model person of exceptional virtue who has died but whose life and works continue to be excellent examples today.*

Sinner: *An unrepentant and incorrigible transgressor whose behaviour and attitudes display the worst excesses of human nature.*

This book is about champions and villains, knights and knaves, and heaven and hell. The myriad centuries of human history have witnessed many brave men and women, and their counterparts: those bent on evil. The purpose of this book is to inspire and entertain readers by detailing the fascinating lives of saints and the appalling activities of notable sinners. How do we even begin to classify and distinguish between the good and disreputable?

Saints are men and women who have lived their lives and received their reward – the kingdom of God. Their exemplary lives provide us with examples to follow so that we may, in turn, follow them to heaven. 'Feast days' are recognized for many saints. These are very often the day of the year in which they died, especially if they gave up their lives for their faith. These special saints who gave up their lives for their faith are called 'martyrs'. Based on the course of their lives and the circumstances surrounding them, some of the saints serve as 'patrons' of certain peoples, places, ailments and occupations, as they intercede for us before God.

If it is difficult to agree on what makes a saint, in theory it should be much easier to recognize a sinner, for we are all sinners. But what marks out a *notable* sinner? Their character, their environment, their upbringing, their friends, or their time in history, perhaps? Are we born bad or made bad? The reality of evil is perhaps the biggest challenge faced by any individual or society.

As I thought through the subject-matter of this book, I decided to adopt a 'big picture' view of what makes a saint and what characterizes a sinner. This means that people and events presented here are what, to my mind, display in sharp relief the character of saints and sinners.

Most of the insights of a saint come from his or her time as a sinner, for that is our natural state. So we see saints not as remote, ephemeral beings, but real people who went through real trials and emerged inspired by God. Sainthood does not take away the human being, but rather enhances the dust – much as particles caught in sunlight achieve a derived brilliance. We are all clay, but we all have the potential to 'shine like stars'.

So, I trust you will enjoy this diversion into the wonderful world of saints and sinners. We are all sinners but with God's grace we may also know the joy of being his saints!

THE EVE OF ST AGNES

Agnes was a fourth-century Christian virgin and martyr, venerated in both the Eastern and Western Churches. Her story is told in the works of St Jerome, Prudentius, St Ambrose and Pope Damasus I, although there are conflicting versions of her martyrdom.

It is thought that when she was about 14, she refused marriage to a host of suitors because of her dedication to Christ. She was denounced as a Christian during the reign of Diocletian and sent to a house of prostitution as her punishment. When a young man ventured to touch her, he lost his sight, but he then regained it in answer to her prayers. Shortly thereafter she was executed and buried on the Via Nomentana in Rome in a catacomb, and a church was built over her tomb about AD 350.

Her feast day is on 21 January and she is often portrayed with a lamb, a symbol of innocence. To this day, each 21 January, two lambs are blessed at her church in Rome. Their wool is then woven into palliums (bands of white wool), which the Pope confers on archbishops as a token of their jurisdiction.

There are lots of stories surrounding the legend of St Agnes and she has been the subject of paintings, songs and a long poem by John Keats written in 1820. It is said that by performing certain rituals, a virgin might see her true love in a dream on the night of 21 January. These rituals include going without supper; reciting the Paternoster while pulling a row of pins from your sleeve; taking sprigs of rosemary and thyme and sprinkling them with water; and placing a shoe on either side of the bed and saying: 'St Agnes, that's to lovers kind, come, ease the trouble of my mind.'

> They told her how, upon St Agnes' Eve,
> Young virgins might have visions of delight,
> And soft adorings from their loves receive
> Upon the honey'd middle of the night,

If ceremonies due they did aright;
As, supperless to bed they must retire,
And couch supine their beauties, lily white;
Nor look behind, nor sideways, but require
Of Heaven with upward eyes for all that they desire.

Extract from 'The Eve of St Agnes' John Keats

And on sweet St Agnes' night
Please you with the promis'd sight,
Some of husbands, some of lovers,
Which an empty dream discovers.

Ben Jonson

STIGMATICS

Stigma (n. pl. stigmata): *Bodily marks, sores or sensations of pain corresponding in location to the crucifixion wounds of Jesus, usually during states of religious ecstasy or hysteria.*

Stigmatics were unknown before the thirteenth century. Although there is no official list of stigmatics, the Catholic Church recognizes 62 saints or blessed men and women as bearing the marks of Christ. Among the best known are:

St Francis of Assisi (1186–1226)
St Lutgarde (1182–1246)
St Margaret of Cortona (1247–97)
St Gertrude (1256–1302)
St Clare of Montefalco (1268–1308)
Bl Angela of Foligno (d. 1309)
St Catherine of Siena (1347–80)
St Lidwine (1380–1433)
St Frances of Rome (1384–1440)
St Colette (1380–1447)

St Rita of Cassia (1386–1456)
Bl Osanna of Mantua (1499–1505)
St Catherine of Genoa (1447–1510)
Bl Baptista Varani (1458–1524)
Bl Lucy of Narni (1476–1547)
Bl Catherine of Racconigi (1486–1547)
St John of God (1495–1550)
St Catherine de' Ricci (1522–89)
St Mary Magdalene de' Pazzi (1566–1607)
Bl Marie de l'Incarnation (1566–1618)
Bl Mary Anne of Jesus (1557–1620)
Bl Carlo of Sezze (d. 1670)
Blessed Margaret Mary Alacoque (1647–90)
St Veronica Giuliani (1600–1727)
St Mary Frances of the Five Wounds (1715–91)
St Pio of Pietrelcina (Padre Pio) (1887–1968)

THE BARBER SAINT

What is so extraordinary about this man? He radiated a most serene and joyful faith. In the face of constant, painful discrimination he understood, as few have understood, the meaning of the words, 'Father, forgive them; they do not know what they are doing.' No treasure is as uplifting and transforming as the light of faith.

Pope John Paul II, 1995

Born a humble, black slave in Haiti in 1776, Pierre Toussaint was elevated to the status of 'Venerable' by the Pope in 1996. Toussaint lived a remarkable life. With no advantages of wealth or background, he learned to read and write because of his kindly master, Jean Berard.

When the Berard family relocated to New York in 1787, Pierre and his sister Rosalie accompanied them. Pierre trained to be a barber and gained a reputation for his tact and discretion. He refused to spread gossip, even though his customers shared with him many confidences. Instead, he would add their concerns to his growing prayer list so that many people were comforted by his untiring dedication.

When his master died, Toussaint could have obtained his freedom, but instead he continued to support his master's family. Eventually, when Mrs Berard remarried, Toussaint set up his own home and married, but had no children.

The Toussaint home became noted as a haven for orphans and the destitute. Pierre purchased freedom for many slaves, gave generously to establish a school for black children, and helped to set up a religious order for black women in Baltimore. He didn't perform miracles, write great books, experience mystical visions or institute a new philosophy. He was an ordinary man, made extraordinary by his faith. Born in the injustice of slavery, Toussaint never allowed his poverty to rob him of his dignity. He rose above racist slurs and ignorant attitudes. He was content to work as a humble barber for God. He did not know the benefits of a privileged birth, but experienced the depths of a generous heart, a confident faith and a close walk with his Saviour.

Toussaint died in 1853 and many poor people who had been helped by his generous life came to pay tribute to him. Today, he is the only layman buried in St Patrick's Cathedral in New York, alongside bishops, cardinals and priests.

Towards the end of his life, Toussaint observed, 'Jesus can give you nothing so precious as himself, as his own mind. Do not think that any faith in him can do you good if you do not try to be pure and true like him.'

THE SAINT MAKER

Archbishop Karol Joseph Wojtyla became Pope John Paul II on 16 October 1978. His death on 2 April 2005 marked the end of the third longest papal reign after Pope Pius IX and the Apostle Peter. Among other things, Pope John Paul II is remembered as a great communicator and tireless traveller, and during his pontificate he canonized more people than any other Pope.

Included in the list of believers made saints by John Paul II are:

Saint	Role	Canonized
Josemaría Escrivá de Balaguer (1902–75)	Founder of Opus Dei	October 2002
Pio da Pietrelcina (1887–1968)	Capuchin priest	June 2002
Edith Stein (1891–1942)	Carmelite martyr	October 1998
Thérèse of Lisieux (1873–97)	Doctor of the Church	June 1997 (originally May 1925)
Maximilian Maria Kolbe (1894–1941)	World War Two martyr	October 1982
Giuseppe Moscati (1880–1927)	Scientist	October 1987
Magdalena of Canossa (1774–1835)	Founder of the of Canossian Family of Daughters and Sons of Charity	October 1988
Clelia Barbieri (1847–70)	Founder of the religious community 'Suore Minime dell'Addolorata'	April 1989

Gaspar Bertoni (1777–1853)	Founder of the Congregationof the Sacred Stigmata of Our Lord Jesus Christ	November 1989
Claudine Thévenet (1774–1837)	Founder of the Congregation of the Religious of Jesus and Mary	March 1993
Hedwig (1374–99)	Queen of Poland	June 1997
John Calabria (1873–1954)	Founder of the Congregation of the Poor Servants and the Poor Women Servants of Divine Providence	April 1999

HOLY NUDISM

The Adamites were an obscure sect that probably originated in North Africa in the second century. They had some strange practices arising from their foundational belief: that they had discovered what life was like before Adam and Eve sinned. They claimed to have returned to a life of innocence before the corruption of sin arising from man's downfall.

Their meetings must have been interesting because they worshipped without clothes (as Adam and Eve had been naked in the Garden of Eden), encouraged freedom of sexual expression and forbade marriage. Their church was called 'paradise', they lived communally, and they frowned upon private possessions.

From North Africa, the sect spread to Spain and Bohemia, but they never gained a large following. In the fourteenth century, the Adamites resurfaced in Eastern Europe as the Brothers and Sisters of the Free Spirit (also known as the

Picards). In the pre-Reformation period, it is thought that the Adamites gradually died out as other sects took hold.

However, in the English Civil War period, around 1650, the Adamites resurfaced again around London. This was a period of great upheaval and their teaching that they were above human laws was attractive to some. They believed they were in a divine state of grace and therefore not beholden to civil, moral or social restraints. It is thought that this sect was dominated by women, but there is scant evidence of their lives from their own accounts. After the Restoration in 1660, the sect died out.

APOSTLE SPOONS

As St Paul's Day, 25 January, is the first feast day of an apostle in the year, it was an old English custom to present spoons (known as apostle spoons) at christenings. The apostle spoons were a gift of 12 spoons with figures of all the apostles on them. Poor people gave one spoon to the child with the figure of the saint after whom the child was named, or to whom the child was dedicated.

This custom is alluded to in Ben Jonson's *Bartholomew Fair*, where a character says, 'And all this for the hope of a couple of apostle-spoons, and a cup to eat caudle in.'

Today these apostle spoons are of considerable value to collectors. The illustration above shows a typical set of such spoons.

FOURTEEN HOLY HELPERS

In the fourteenth century, the Black Plague devastated Europe and many died without receiving the last sacraments. It was a violent time, and those with the disease were often attacked and segregated.

Many people invoked a group of saints known as the Fourteen Holy Helpers during the Black Plague. Their devotion began in Germany and spread throughout most of Europe during the fourteenth century. The Fourteen Holy Helpers collectively venerated on 8 August every year were:

Saint	Condition
Achatius	Headaches
Barbara	Fevers, sudden death
Blaise	Ills of the throat
Catherine of Alexandria	Sudden death
Christopher	Plagues, sudden death
Cyriacus	Temptation
Denis	Headaches
George	Protection of domestic animals
Giles	Plagues
Margaret of Antioch	For safe childbirth
Pantaleon	Protection of domestic animals
Vitus	Epilepsy
Erasmus	Intestinal trouble
Eustachius	Difficult situations

Invocation of the Holy Helpers

Fourteen Holy Helpers, who served God in humility and confidence on earth and are now in the enjoyment of His beatific vision in Heaven; because thou persevered till death thou gained the crown of eternal life. Remember the dangers that surround us in this vale of tears, and intercede for us in all our needs and adversities. Amen.

Fourteen Holy Helpers, select friends of God, I honour thee as mighty intercessors, and come with filial confidence to thee in my needs, for the relief of which I have undertaken to make this novena. Help me by thy intercession to placate God's wrath, which I have provoked by my sins, and aid me in amending my life and doing penance. Obtain for me the grace to serve God with a willing heart, to be resigned to His holy will, to be patient in adversity and to persevere unto the end, so that, having finished my earthly course, I may join thee in Heaven, there to praise for ever God, who is wonderful in His Saints. Amen.

Catholic Encyclopaedia, *Robert Appleton, 1907*

NUREMBERG TRIALS

After World War II, on 20 November 1945, the Allies convened an International Military Tribunal at the Palace of Justice in Nuremberg, in Germany, to prosecute Nazi war criminals.

The indictment that served as the basis for the trials and for charging the defendants contained four counts:

Count One – The Common Plan or Conspiracy to wage a aggressive war in violation of international law or treaties.

Count Two – Planning, preparation, or waging an aggressive war.

Count Three – War Crimes – violations of the international rules of war (mistreatment of prisoners of war or civilian populations, the plunder of private property and the destruction of towns and cities without military justification).

Count Four – Crimes Against Humanity – murder, exterm-
ination, enslavement of civilian populations; persecution on
the basis of racial, religious or political grounds.

The defendants (and their fate) are:

Name	Fate
Hermann Goering	Sentenced to death, but committed suicide
Rudolph Hess	Life imprisonment – committed suicide in 1987
Hans Frank	Sentenced to death
Wilhelm Frick	Sentenced to death
Julius Streicher	Sentenced to death
Walther Funk	Life imprisonment – died in 1960
Fritz Sauckel	Sentenced to death
Alfred Jodl	Sentenced to death
Martin Bormann	Sentenced to death (in absentia)
Franz von Papen	Acquitted
Joachim von Ribbentrop	Sentenced to death
Wilhelm Keitel	Sentenced to death
Ernst Kaltenbrunner	Sentenced to death
Alfred Rosenberg	Sentenced to death
Hjalmar Schacht	Acquitted
Karl Doenitz	10 years' imprisonment
Erich Raeder	Life imprisonment
Baldur von Schirach	20 years' imprisonment
Arthur Seyss-Inquart	Sentenced to death
Albert Speer	20 years' imprisonment
Konstantin von Neurath	15 years' imprisonment
Hans Fritzsche	Acquitted

The Trials concluded on 1 October 1946, the Jewish Day of Atonement.

WITCHCRAFT IN SALEM COUNTY

The principal parties accused of witchcraft in Salem County, Massachusetts, in 1692 and their fate were:

Accused	Sentence
Sarah Osborn	Died in prison
Roger Toothaker	Died in prison
Lydia Dustin	Died in prison
Ann Foster	Died in prison
Bridget Bishop	Executed 10 June 1692
Rebecca Nurse	Executed 19 July 1692
Sarah Good	Executed 19 July 1692
Susannah Martin	Executed 19 July 1692
Elizabeth Howe	Executed 19 July 1692
Sarah Wildes	Executed 19 July 1692
John Willard	Executed 19 August 1692
George Jacobs, Sr	Executed 19 August 1692
John Proctor	Executed 19 August 1692
George Burroughs	Executed 19 August 1692
Martha Carrier	Executed 19 August 1692
Giles Corey	Pressed to death 16 September 1692
Marth Corey	Executed 22 September 1692
Mary Easty	Executed 22 September 1692
Ann Pudeator	Executed 22 September 1692
Alice Parker	Executed 22 September 1692

Mary Parker	Executed 22 September 1692
Wilmott Redd	Executed 22 September 1692
Margaret Scott	Executed 22 September 1692
Samuel Wardwell	Executed 22 September 1692

'SAINTS GO MALTING IN'

It is strange to note that many saints have ancient connections with the production of beer. Here is a list of saints and their links with beer:

Saint	Brewing link
Lawrence	He suffered martyrdom in 258 by being strapped to a grid iron that was slowly roasted over an open flame. He is remembered by brewers because this is how malt is dried.
Dorothy	Died in 311 after undergoing similar tortures to St Lawrence. Remembered for the same reason by brewers.
Augustine of Hippo	Known for his wild living (including drunkenness) prior to his conversion. He is the patron saint of brewers.
Luke the Apostle	Another patron of brewers, possibly due to his being a doctor and recommending beer as a useful medium in which to mix herbs for medicinal purposes.
Nicholas of Myra	The model for Santa Claus is supposed to have revived three church scholars in an inn. He is therefore the protector of travellers and brewers.

Wenceslas	Said to have imposed the death penalty on anyone caught exporting Bohemian hops. Remembered by hop-growers, and is the patron saint of Czech brewers. He is the ancestor of Wenceslas II who, in the thirteenth century, convinced the Pope to lift the ban on the brewing of beer.
Veronus	The patron saint of Belgian brewers.
Brigid	She is supposed to have bathed lepers in beer.
Amand	Considered the father of Belgian monasticism, he established many beer-producing monasteries across northern France and Belgium.
Gambrinus	The legendary King of Flanders, he is also known as the 'King of Beer', for reputedly inventing hopped, malt beer.
Arnold of Soissons	The patron saint of hop pickers because he preached in the hop-laden areas of Brabant.
Arnold of Metz	According to legend, he ended a plague when he submerged his crucifix into a brew kettle and persuaded people to drink only beer from that 'blessed' kettle. He is reported to have said, 'From man's sweat and God's love, beer came into the world'.

FAMOUS FRAUDSTERS

'Count' Victor Lustig	In 1925 he tried to sell the Eiffel Tower to scrap merchants.
Frank Abagnale	Famous forger and impersonator, portrayed by Leonardo di Caprio in the film *Catch Me If You Can*.
Marmaduke Wetherell and Colonel Robert Wilson	Responsible for the famous fake Loch Ness Monster photo.
Charles Ponzi	Inventor of the 'pyramid scheme'.
Joseph 'Yellow Kid' Weil	The inspiration for hit film *The Sting*.
Clifford Irving	Fake 'autobiography' of Howard Hughes.
John Stonehouse	UK politician who faked his own death in 1974.
Charles Dawson	Piltdown Man hoax.
George Hull	Fake prehistoric figure, the Cardiff Giant.
Mahzer Mahmood	Fake 'Tabloid' sheik who had conversations with Sophie Rhys-Jones, wife of Prince Edward.
Charles Redheffer	Inventor of a perpetual motion machine.
Mary Baker	Fake Oriental – Princess Caraboo.
William Henry Ireland	Faked Shakespeare's relics.
Frances Griffiths and Elsie Wright	Photographed the so-called Cottingley Fairies.

Richard Dimbleby	Presenter of the famous April Fool's joke of the Swiss spaghetti harvest on *Panorama* in 1957.
Konrad Kujau	Fake Hitler diaries.

THE GOVERNMENT OF HADES

In 1583, German physician and occultist Johannes Wierus published a major work called *Pseudomonarchia Daemonum*, which attempted to detail the Government of Hades. According to Wierus, the chief emperor of the demons was Belzebuth or Belzebub. He is said to have been worshipped by the people of Canaan in the form of a fly, and hence believed to have founded the Order of the Fly. Wierus claimed that Satan, the former emperor, had been usurped and was now the leader of the opposition.

Wierus included the following evil spirits in the Government of Hades:

Name	Title
Eurynome	Prince of Death
Moloch	Prince of the Country of Tears
Pluto	Prince of Fire
Baalberith	Secretary General of the Archives of Hell
Prosperine	Princess of Evil Spirits
Belphegor	Hadean Ambassador to France
Mammon	Hadean Ambassador to England
Belial	Hadean Ambassador to Turkey
Rimmon	Hadean Ambassador to Russia
Thammuz	Hadean Ambassador to Spain
Hutgin	Hadean Ambassador to Italy

Martinet	Hadean Ambassador to Switzerland
Lucifer	Minister of Justice
Alastor	Executioner

Wierus calculated that Belzebuth's Empire had 6,666 legions, each composed of 6,666 demons, giving a Hadean population of over 44 million.

JOSEPH SCRIVEN

Joseph Scriven was the author of the popular hymn 'What a Friend We Have in Jesus'. An exemplary Christian, born in Ireland in 1819, Scriven emigrated to Canada following a tragedy. He was due to marry a local girl, but in 1842, on the eve of their wedding, his fiancée drowned in the River Bann after falling from her horse.

The incident that inspired the hymn occurred in 1854. Joseph was again due to be married in 1854 to Elizabeth Roche. Unfortunately, she caught a chill, became seriously ill, and died after suffering for three years. Scriven was extremely moved by these events and wrote the hymn orginally as a poem for his mother in 1857. It was originally called 'Pray Without Ceasing' .

What a Friend We Have in Jesus

What a friend we have in Jesus,
All our sins and griefs to bear!
What a privilege to carry
Everything to God in prayer!
O what peace we often forfeit,
O what needless pain we bear,
All because we do not carry
Everything to God in prayer.

Have we trials and temptations?
   Is there trouble anywhere?
We should never be discouraged
   Take it to the Lord in prayer!
Can we find a friend so faithful,
Who will all our sorrows share?
Jesus knows our every weakness
   Take it to the Lord in prayer!

Are we weak and heavy laden,
Cumbered with a load of care?
Precious Saviour, still our refuge
   Take it to the Lord in prayer.
Do your friends despise forsake you?
   Take it to the Lord in prayer!
In His arms He'll take and shield you
   You will find a solace there.

SAINTS AND WEATHER LORE

St Vincent's Day – 22 January

St Vincent was a Spanish martyr who died in 304 after suffering torture by fire. An ancient proverb says that if the sun is out on St Vincent's Day, then it will continue to shine throughout the rest of the month:

Remember on St Vincent's Day
If that the sun his beams display.

St Paul's Day – 25 January

According to *Every-Day Book*, 1825–7, 'On this day prognostications of the months were drawn for the whole year. If fair and clear, there was to be plenty; if cloudy or misty, much cattle would die; if rain or snow fell then it presaged a dearth; and if windy, there would be wars:'

> If Saint Paul's Day be fair and clear.
> It does betide a happy year;
> But if it chance to snow or rain,
> Then will be dear all kinds of grain:
> If clouds or mists do dark the skie,
> Great store of birds and beasts shall die;
> And if the winds do fly aloft,
> Then wars shall vex the kingdome oft.

Candlemass Day – 2 February

This feast day celebrates the purification of the Virgin Mary, 40 days after the birth of Jesus. The weather on this day is said to mark the progress of winter according to the rhyme:

> If the sun shines bright on Candlemass Day
> The half of Winter's not yet away

St Winwaloe's Day – 3 March

St Winwaloe's Day is associated with storms, according to this rhyme:

> First there's David
> Then there's Chad
> Next comes Winwaloe
> Roaring mad

St Medard's Day – 8 June

> Should Saint Medard's day be wet
> It will rain for forty yet;
> At least until Saint Barnabas

The summer sun won't favour us,
If on the eighth of June it rain,
It foretells a wet harvest, men sain.

Saints Gervasius and Protasius – 19 June

S'il pleut le jour de Saint Médard,
Il pleut quarante jours plus tard;
S'il pleut le jour de Saint Gervais
    et de Saint Protais,
Il pleut quarante jours après.

St Swithin's Day – 15 July

In this month is St Swithin's Day;
On which, if that it rain, they say
Full forty days after it will,
Or more or less, some rain distill.
This Swithin was a saint, I trow,
And Winchester's bishop also.
Who in his time did many a feat,
As popish legends do repeat:
A woman having broke her eggs
By stumbling at another's legs,
For which she made a woful cry,
St Swithin chanc'd for to come by,
Who made them all as sound, or more
Than ever that they were before.
But whether this were so or no
'Tis more than you or I do know:
Better it is to rise betime,
And to make hay while sun doth shine,
Than to believe in tales and lies
Which idle monks and friars devise.

St James's Day – 25 July

If it be fair three Sundays before St James Day, corn will be good; but wet corn will wither

St Andrew's Day – 30 November

According to an old country saying, *'St Andrew's snow to corn works woe'*

Hone's Every-Day Book, *1825–27*

DOCTORS OF THE CHURCH

The Catholic Church proclaims a person to be a Doctor of the Church if they meet three requirements according to Pope Benedict XIV's definition: an eminent doctrine, a remarkable holiness of life, and the declaration by the Supreme Pontiff or by a General Council.

Below is a list of Doctors of the Church, starting with their name(s), the Pope who proclaimed them, and the date on which this occurred:

- 1–4: Saints Ambrose, Jerome, Augustine, Gregory the Great: Boniface VIII, 20 September 1295.
- 5: Saint Thomas Aquinas: Saint Pius V, 11 April 1567.
- 6–9: Saints Athanasius, Basil, Gregory of Nazianzus, Saint John Chrysostom: Saint Pius V, 1568.
- 10: Saint Bonaventure: Sixtus V, 14 March 1588.
- 11: Saint Anselm of Canterbury: Clement XI, 3 February 1720.
- 12: Saint Isidore of Seville: Innocent XIII, 25 April 1722.
- 13: Saint Peter Chrysologus: Benedict XIII, 10 February 1729.
- 14: Saint Leo the Great: Benedict XIV, 15 October 1754.
- 15: Saint Peter Damian: Leo XII, 27 September 1828.
- 16: Saint Bernard of Clairvaux: Pius VIII, 20 August 1830.
- 17: Saint Hilaire of Poitiers: Pius IX, 13 May 1851.
- 18: Saint Alphonsus Liguori: Pius IX, 7 July 1871.

- 19: Saint Francis of Sales: Pius IX, 16 November 1871.
- 20–21: Saints Cyril of Alexandria and Cyril of Jerusalem: Leo XIII, 28 July 1882.
- 22: Saint John Damascene: Leo XIII, 19 August 1890.
- 23: Saint Bede the Venerable: Leo XIII, 13 November 1899.
- 24: Saint Ephrem of Syria: Benedict XV, 5 October 1920.
- 25: Saint Peter Canisius: Pius XI, 21 May 1925.
- 26: Saint John of the Cross: Pius XI, 24 August 1926.
- 27: Saint Robert Bellarmine: Pius XI, 17 September 1931.
- 28: Saint Albert the Great: Pius XI, 16 December 1931.
- 29: Saint Antony of Padua: Pius XII, 16 January 1946.
- 30: Saint Laurence of Brindisi: John XXIII, 19 March 1959.
- 31: Saint Teresa of Avila: Paul VI, 27 September 1970.
- 32: Saint Catherine of Siena: Paul VI, 4 October 1970.
- 33: Saint Thérèse of Lisieux: John Paul II, 19 October 1997.

CURIOUS SAINTS DAY CUSTOMS

- In Scotland, on the eve of St Andrew's Day (29 November), the traditional sport was squirrel hunting. This 'Andermas' custom was transported to the colonies and still survives in some parts of the Commonwealth.
- In Poland, if there is a red sunset on St Nicholas's Day (6 December), it is thought that angels are making his favourite honey cakes.
- Assumption Day (15 August) is reckoned to be an excellent time for betrothals in Brittany.
- In Spain, on St Giles's Day (1 September) rams were dyed in bright colours and blessed in special church services. As well as being the saint of cripples, St Giles is also known as the protector of rams.
- On St George's Day (23 April), races, processions and jousts were held in medieval England.
- On St Hugh's Day (1 April), mock turtle soup is traditionally eaten in Switzerland. This recalls the saint's transformation of a bowl of fowl into turtles!

- Traditionally, Welshmen wear leeks in their hats on St David's Day (1 March).
- In the Middle Ages, it was thought that birds began to mate on St Valentine's Day (14 February).
- Sheaves of corn used to be hung decoratively over church doors on Lammas Day (1 August) – the feast of St Peter – to mark the reaping of the first fruits.

SAINT-RELATED PHRASES

St Andrew's Cross	An X-shaped cross, like the one upon which St Andrew suffered martyrdom. Also the name of a low-growing North American shrub.
St Antony's Cross	A T-shaped cross, like the one upon which St Antony suffered martyrdom.
St Antony's Fire	An acute inflammatory skin disease, so called because St Antony was supposed to have cured a sufferer from it. Also known as erysipelas.
St Antony's Nut	*Conopodium mais,* a groundnut used for swinefeed. St Antony was once a swineherd.
St Antony's Turnip	Another favourite food of swine, popularly known as the bulbous crowfoot.
St Barnaby's Thistle	Supposed to flower on St Barnabas's Day (11 June), this is a kind of knapweed (*Centaurea solstitialis).*
St Catherine's Flower	The plant commonly known as 'love in a mist'.

St Cuthbert's Beads	A paleontological term used to describe the crinoid stems of fossil joints.
St Cuthbert's Duck	A species of eider duck.
St Dabeoc's Heath	Named after an Irish saint, this is a heather-like plant found in Ireland (*Daboecia polifolia*).
St David's Herb	*Allium porrum*, the leek is David's emblem.
St Distaff's Day	Also known as Rock Day, this is the day after Epiphany (7 January). So called because it marked the day when work began after the Christmas feast.
St Elmo's Fire	A luminous flame seen on a ship, probably caused by a discharge of electricity. St Elmo is the patron of sailors.
St George's Ensign	A red cross on a white field with the Union Jack in the upper corner next to the mast. It is the badge of the English Royal Navy.
St George's Flag	A red cross upon a white field. Its presence on a ship is used to indicate that the vessel is under the command of an admiral.
St George's Flower	*Endymion non-scriptus,* the blue-bell that reaches its peak around St George's Day, 23 April.
St George's Herb	The plant commonly known as valerian.
St Gregory's Fig	*Ficus carica* – figs were given on St Gregory's Day to schoolchildren at the Free School in Giggleswick, Yorkshire.

St Ignatius's Bean	The seed from a tree native to the Philippines (*Strychnos ignatia*).
St James's Shell	A comb (pecten) worn by pilgrims to Compostella.
St James's Wort	A kind of ragwort (*Senecio jacobaea*).
St John's Bread	*Ceratonia siliqua,* the locust tree or carob.
St John's Wort	Any plant of the genus *Hypericum*.
St Joseph's Flower	*Althaea rosea,* Holyoake – traditionally planted on St Joseph's Day
St Johnstone's Tippet	Hangman's noose.
St Leger	A horse race named after Colonel St Leger.
St Martin's Herb	A medicinal herb from Latin America, *Sayvagesia erecta*.
St Michael's Chair	Stone feature on St Michael's Mount in Cornwall.
St Monday	Day of idleness observed by workers such as shoemakers and merchants.

ALL SAINTS' DAY

This day honours all saints of the Church, even those not known by name. The first All Saints' Day occurred on 13 May AD 609, although Ephrem Syrus mentions a feast dedicated to saints taking place in the fourth century. In the same century, St Chrysostom of Constantinople assigned All Saints' Day to the first Sunday after Pentecost. It was not recognized in the Western Church, however, until the Roman bishop

Boniface IV consecrated the Pantheon at Rome to Christian usage as a church on 13 May 609. All Saints' Day was observed annually on this date until Pope Gregory III changed the date to 1 November, since on this date he dedicated a chapel in the Basilica of St Peter's to 'All the Saints' in the seventh century. The Orthodox Churches still observe All Saints Day on the first Sunday after Pentecost.

All Saints Day is celebrated by Roman Catholics, Orthodox Churches, Anglicans and Lutherans. However, different denominations celebrate the day for different reasons. For Roman Catholics, Orthodox Churches and, to some extent, Anglicans, All Saints' Day is a day to venerate and pray to the saints in heaven. For Lutherans, the day is observed by remembering and thanking God for all saints, both dead and living.

FAMOUS SAINTS' PRAYERS

A Prayer of St Francis

Lord, make me an instrument of thy peace,
Where there is hatred, let me sow love;
Where there is injury, pardon;
Where there is doubt, faith;
Where there is despair, hope;
Where there is darkness, light;
Where there is sadness, joy.
O Divine Master,
Grant that I may not so much seek
To be consoled, as to console;
To be understood, as to understand;
To be loved, as to love;
For it is in giving that we receive;
It is in pardoning that we are pardoned;
And it is in dying that we are
born to eternal life. Amen.

St Patrick's Breastplate

May the strength of God pilot us.
May the power of God preserve us.
May the wisdom of God instruct us.
May the hand of God protect us.
May the way of God direct us.
May the shield of God defend us,
May the host of God guard us
Against the snares of evil
    and the temptations of the world.
May Christ be with us, Christ before us,
Christ in us, Christ over us.
May thy salvation, O Lord, be always ours
this day and evermore.

St Anselm's Prayer

O Lord our God, grant us grace to desire thee with our
    whole heart;
that so desiring, we may seek and find thee;
and finding thee, we may love thee;
and loving thee, we may hate those sins from which thou
    hast redeemed us.

Ignatius Loyola's Prayer

Teach us, good Lord, to serve thee as thou deservest;
to give and not to count the cost;
to fight and not to heed the wounds;
to toil and not to seek for rest;
to labour and not to ask for any reward,
save that of knowing we do thy will. Amen.

CLASSIFICATION OF SAINTS

Orthodox Church classification:

Apostles	Those who were chosen by Jesus and witnessed his ministry.
Prophets	Those who predicted the coming of the Messiah.
Martyrs	Those who sacrifice their lives for their faith in Christ.
Church Fathers	Those who excel in explaining and defending the faith.
Monastics	Desert dwellers dedicated to spiritual excellence.
Just	Those who live exemplary lives in testimony to Christ.

BECOMING A SAINT

In the Catholic Church, canonization – the process the Church uses to elect a saint – was clarified by Pope John Paul II in 1983. Previously, saints were chosen by public acclaim. Though this was a more democratic way to recognize saints, some saints' stories were distorted by legend and some supposed saints never existed. As a result, gradually the bishops – and finally the Vatican – took over authority for canonization.

Today, canonization begins after the death of a Catholic whom people regard as holy. Often, the process starts many years after their death in order to give perspective to the candidate. The local bishop investigates the candidate's life and writings for heroic virtue (or martyrdom) and orthodoxy of doctrine. Then a panel of theologians at the Vatican evaluates the candidate. Upon the recommendation of the panel and cardinals of the Congregation for the Causes of Saints, the Pope proclaims the candidate *venerable*.

The next step, *beatification*, requires evidence of one miracle (except in the case of martyrs). Since miracles are considered proof that the person is in heaven and can intercede for us, the miracle must take place after the candidate's death and as a result of a specific petition to the candidate. When the Pope proclaims the candidate beatified or 'blessed', the person can be venerated by a particular region or group of people for whom the person holds special importance.

After one more miracle the Pope will canonize the saint (this includes martyrs as well). The title of 'saint' tells us that the person lived a holy life, is in heaven, and is to be honoured by the Church.

Though canonization is infallible and irrevocable, it takes a long time and a lot of effort. So while every person who is canonized is a saint, not every holy person has been canonized.

LAST WORDS AT EXECUTION

You are going to hurt me, please don't hurt me, just one more moment, I beg you!

[*Guillotined*] – Madame du Barry, mistress of Louis XV, d. 1793

Take a step forward, lads. It will be easier that way.

[*Executed by firing squad*] – Erskine Childers, Irish patriot, d. 24 November 1922

Such is life

[*Executed by hanging*] – Ned Kelly, Australian bushranger, d. 1880

Farewell, my children, forever. I go to your Father.

[*Executed by guillotine*]
Monsieur, I beg your pardon.

[*Spoken to the executioner, after she stepped on his foot*] –
Marie Antoinette, Queen of France, d. 16 October 1793

Shoot me in the chest!

[*To his executioners*] – Benito Mussolini, Italian dictator,
d. 1945

So the heart be right, it is no matter which way the head
lieth.

[*Executed by beheading*] – Sir Walter Raleigh, d. 29 October
1618

OUR LADY OF HATRED

(Fr. Notre-Dame de la Haine)

The name popularly given to a church in Treguier, Brittany.
Souvestre, in his *Derniers Bretons*, vol. i, p. 92, tells us that
'hither come at even-tide young people tired of the surveillance
of their elders, old men envious of the prosperity of their
neighbours, wives chafing under the despotism of their
husbands, each praying for the death of the object of their
hate. Three Aves, devoutly repeated, will bring about this
death within the twelve-month.'

Curiosities of Popular Customs and of Rites, Ceremonies,
Observances, and Miscellaneous Antiquities, *William S. Walsh, J. B.
Lippincott Company*, 1852

Anthony Trollope's older brother, Thomas, wrote many
novels, mostly based in Italy. His autobiography, *What I
Remember* (1887), contrasts some of his recollections of child-

hood with those of his younger brother Anthony. This is his account of his visit to Brittany, where he too heard about Our Lady of Hatred.

Very near Treguier, on a spot appropriately selected for such a worship – the barren top of a bleak unsheltered eminence – stands the chapel of Notre Dame de la Haine! Our Lady of HATRED! The most fiendish of human passions is supposed to be under the protection of Christ's religion! What is this but a fragment of pure and unmixed Paganism, unchanged except in the appellation of its idol, which has remained among these lineal descendants of the Armorican Druids for more than a thousand years after Christianity has become the professed religion of the country! Altars, professedly Christian, were raised under the protection of the Protean Virgin, to the demon Hatred; and have continued to the present day to receive an unholy worship from blinded bigots, who hope to obtain Heaven's patronage and assistance for thoughts and wishes which they would be ashamed to breathe to man. Three Aves repeated with devotion at this odious and melancholy shrine are firmly believed to have the power to cause, within the year, the certain death of the person against whom the assistance of Our Lady of Hatred has been invoked. And it is said that even yet occasionally, in the silence and obscurity of the evening, the figure of some assassin worshipper at this accursed shrine may be seen to glide rapidly from the solitary spot, where he has spoken the unhallowed prayer whose mystic might has doomed to death the enemy he hates.

What I Remember, *Thomas Adolphous Trollope, 1887*

THE WICKED LADY

Katherine Ferrers, lady by day, highway robber by night, and known as the 'Wicked Lady', has been the subject of fascination for over 300 years. Born in 1634 during the English Civil War, Ferrers was heir to a large fortune until she was cheated out of it by circumstances beyond her control.

Her father, Knighton Ferrers, died just two weeks before she was born. Her mother, Lady Katherine Walters of Hertingford, remarried Sir Simon Fanshaw, a noted royalist, who purloined the family fortune and had to go into hiding in Europe. Thus Katherine Ferrers was denied her family inheritance.

According to legend, around 1652 Katherine met a farmer, Ralph Chaplin, who was a highwayman by night. She joined Chaplin and wrought havoc on travellers in the Hertfordshire countryside. One night, Chaplin was caught committing a robbery and executed on the spot.

Lady Katherine Ferrers became a solitary robber dressed in highwayman's garb: a three-cornered hat, a black mask, black riding cloak, scarf and breeches, and rode a black horse with white flashes on its forelegs. She would change at dusk into her highwayman's clothes in a secret room in her house, accessed through a concealed staircase. She did not use the standard 'Stand and deliver' charge to her victims, but emerged from the darkness to ruthlessly attack coachmen and passengers alike. Yet nobody, not even her servants, knew of Katherine's misdeeds.

Lady Katherine has been caricatured as a pretty young woman wearing a black mask over her eyes, perhaps with a roguish smile, or simply as a stereotyped masked highwayman, indistinguishable from her male peers. Always there is the gun and the three-cornered hat.

Among the crimes attributed to the Wicked Lady were murder, robbery, arson, cattle who were shot in the fields, and a policeman who was shot dead on his own doorstep.

The Wicked Lady died childless in 1660 and was buried in Ware, Hertfordshire.

Her story has been the basis of at least two films, a novel by Sir Walter Scott and countless ballads. It is said that the ghost of the Wicked Lady can be still seen today as a figure astride a galloping black horse in the Hertfordshire countryside on bleak winter nights.

PRINCIPAL NATIONAL SAINTS

Nation	Saint	Memorial Day
Albania	Our Lady of Good Counsel	26 April
Algeria	Cyprian of Carthage	16 September
Angola	Immaculate Heart of Mary	22 August
Argentina	Francis Solano	14 July
Armenia	Gregory the Illuminator	30 September
Australia	Francis Xavier	3 December
Austria	Florian	4 May
Belgium	Columbanus of Ghent	2 February
Bolivia	Francis Solano	14 July
Brazil	Antony of Padua	13 June
Bulgaria	Cyril the Philosopher	14 February
Chile	Francis Solano	14 July
China	Francis Xavier	3 December
Costa Rica	Our Lady of The Angels	2 August
Cuba	Our Lady of Charity of El Cobre	8 September
Cyprus	Barnabas the Apostle	11 June
Czech Rep.	Wenceslas	28 September
Denmark	Canute	19 January
Dominican Rep.	Dominic de Guzman	8 August
Egypt	Mark the Evangelist	25 April

Ethiopia	Frumentius	27 October
England	George	23 April
France	Joan of Arc	30 May
Germany	Boniface	5 June
Gibraltar	Bernard of Clairvaux	20 August
Greece	Andrew the Apostle	30 November
Guatemala	James the Greater	25 July
Haiti	Our Lady of Perpetual Help	27 June
Hungary	Astricus	12 November
Iceland	Thorlac Thorhallsson	23 December
India	Thomas the Apostle	3 July
Iran	Maruthas	4 December
Ireland	Patrick	17 March
Italy	Our Lady of Perpetual Help	27 June
Jamaica	Mary of the Assumption	15 August
Japan	Francis Xavier	3 December
Jordan	John the Baptist	24 June
Korea	Joseph the Betrothed	19 March
Lithuania	Casimir of Poland	4 March
Luxembourg	Philip the Apostle	3 May
Madagascar	Vincent de Paul	27 September
Malta	Paul the Apostle	25 January
Mexico	Elias del Socorro Nieves	10 March
Netherlands	Bavo	1 October

New Zealand	Francis Xavier	3 December
Nicaragua	James the Greater	25 July
Nigeria	Patrick	17 March
Norway	Olaf II	29 July
Pakistan	Thomas the Apostle	3 July
Papua New Guinea	Michael the Archangel	29 September
Paraguay	Francis Solano	14 July
Peru	Francis Solano	14 July
Philippines	Rose of Lima	23 August
Poland	Casimir of Poland	4 March
Romania	Nicetas	7 January
Russia	Andrew the Apostle	30 November
Scotland	Andrew the Apostle	30 November
Serbia	Sava	14 January
Slovakia	Our Lady of Sorrows	15 September
Spain	James the Greater	25 July
Sri Lanka	Lawrence	10 August
Sudan	Josephine Bakhita	8 February
Sweden	Bridget of Sweden	23 July
Switzerland	Gall	16 Octobe
Syria	Barbara	4 December
Ukraine	Josaphat	12 November
USA	Immaculate Conception of Mary	8 December
Wales	David	1 March
West Indies	Rose of Lima	23 August

CURIOUS SAINTLY DEEDS
– PART ONE

- St Antony of Padua once preached to fishes in the Italian town of Rimini because he was so disheartened by the stubborn hearts of the local people.

- In 1884, Pope Leo XIII claimed to have heard a conversation between the Lord and the Devil. He wrote this prayer to St Michael the Archangel after this experience: 'St Michael the Archangel, defend us in the day of battle, be our safeguard against the wickedness and snares of the Devil. May God rebuke him, we humbly pray, and do you the Prince of the Heavenly Host, by the power of God cast into hell Satan and all the other evil spirits, who prowl throughout the world, seeking the ruination of men, Amen.'

- When Attila the Hun was about to invade Paris, St Geneviève urged the townspeople to fast, repent and pray. The threatened invasion never took place.

- On 26 December 1944 (the feast day of the first martyr, St Stephen), Karl Leisner, a Catholic priest, celebrated Mass in a Nazi concentration camp in defiance of the authorities. Shortly afterwards, he was executed. In 1996, he was made a saint.

- St Fabian inadvertently became Pope for 16 years when he wandered into a papal election meeting. A dove descended on his head and the Council took this to be a divine sign that Fabian should be Pope.

- In order to distract himself from impure thoughts at a local dance, St Wulfstan threw himself into a thicket of thorns and thistles. He was never bothered with impure thoughts again.

- St Angela Merici was struck with sudden blindness in 1524 in Crete on her way to the Holy Land. She nevertheless insisted on continuing her journey and experienced a sightless pilgrimage. On her return journey, her sight was restored in Crete.

- St Rose of Lima rubbed her face with pepper because she was too good looking.

- St Maria de la Cabeza's head used to be paraded at the head of a procession in Spain during times of drought.

- St John of the Cross died while in prayer in 1591. In 1926, 335 years later, his body was exhumed to be relocated in a special shrine in his honour. It was found to be remarkably preserved, showing little sign of decay. It was even flexible.

JESUS DAY

In 2000, Texas Governor George W. Bush declared 10 June to be officially recognized as Jesus Day. This is his proclamation (from the Texas State Archives):

OFFICIAL MEMORANDUM
STATE OF TEXAS
OFFICE OF THE GOVERNOR

Throughout the world, people of all religions recognize Jesus Christ as an example of love, compassion, sacrifice and service. Reaching out to the poor, the suffering and the marginalized, he provided moral leadership that continues to inspire countless men, women and children today.

To honor his life and teachings, Christians of all races and denominations have joined together to designate June 10 as Jesus Day. As part of this celebration of unity, they are taking part in the 10th annual March for Jesus in cities throughout the Lone Star State. The march, which began in Austin in 1991, is now held in nearly 180 countries. Jesus Day challenges people to follow Christ's example by performing good works in their communities and neighborhoods. By nursing the sick, feeding the poor or volunteering in homeless shelters, everyone can play a role in making the world a better place.

I urge all Texans to answer the call to serve those in need. By volunteering their time, energy or resources to helping others, adults and youngsters follow Christ's message of love and service in thought and in deed.

Therefore, I, George W. Bush, Governor of Texas, do hereby proclaim June 10 2000

JESUS DAY

Jesus Day takes place each year on the Saturday before Pentecost Sunday, hence the date is not fixed. In 2005, Jesus Day was on 14 May with the theme, 'Created to Love, Called to Serve'.

HYPERDULIA

The Virgin Mary is the most venerated saint and there are numerous forms of piety towards the Mother of God. The term *hyperdulia* refers to the special reverence of Mary. It is the second highest form of reverence permitted in the Catholic Church. *Latria* is the highest reverence, reserved for God alone, and below *hyperdulia* is *dulia*, which is reverence for all the heavenly host.

DE-CANONIZED SAINTS

From the 1960s onwards, after Vatican II, the Catholic Church 'de-canonized' some saints because of lack of evidence about their lives (whether they even existed) and their deeds (whether they performed miracles). Examples of de-canonization include:

- *St Barbara* – possibly an apocryphal saint of either Greek, Italian or Egyptian birth! The dates surrounding her life are uncertain and, as a result of lack of information, she was de-canonized in 1969.

- *Simon of Trent* was canonized in the thirteenth century, but de-canonized in 1965 because of lack of evidence.

- *St Brigit* was de-canonized because she was originally thought to be a pagan goddess, worshipped by the Celts at Kildare in the thirteenth century.

There is some dispute about whether the popular saints, Christopher, Valentine, George, Philomena and Thomas Beckett, are still official saints or whether they have been de-canonized because of the greater number of legendary tales about their lives.

THE WORLD'S WORST DICTATORS

Dictator-watcher David Wallechinsky, in collaboration with Amnesty International, Freedom House, Human Rights Watch and Reporters Without Borders, compiled the following list of the world's worst dictators (2003).

Country	Dictator	Comments
North Korea	1 Kim Jong II	In power since 1994, aka 'The Beloved Leader'.
Burma	2 Than Shwe	Sole leader of military dictatorship since 1991.

China	3 Hu Jintao	China executes more people than the rest of the world put together.
Zimbabwe	4 Robert Mugabe	More than 70,000 people have been killed, tortured or displaced by his regime.
Saudi Arabia	5 Prince Abdullah	More than 8 million foreigners suffer 'slavery-like' conditions.
Equatorial Guinea	6 Teodoro Nguema	More than half the population survive on 60p a day.
Sudan	7 Omar Al Bashir	2 million killed and 4 million homeless from the 20-year civil war.
Turkmenistan	8 Saparmurat Niyazov	Beards, gold teeth and circuses banned. Months of the year named after his mother.
Cuba	9 Fidel Castro	Longest surviving dictator.
Swaziland	10 King Mswati III	Some 300,000 drought-stricken farmers left to suffer starvation.

BLESSING THE THROAT

In many Roman Catholic churches, the lovely ceremony of Blessing the Throat is performed on St Blaise's Day – 3 February. Two long candles are blessed and lit in the form of a St Andrew's Cross. Sufferers from throat ailments kneel while the ribboned cross is laid under their chins and their throats are gently stroked with the ends of the candles. As the candles touch the sufferers, the priest says to each in turn, 'May the Lord deliver you from the evil of the throat, and from every other evil.'

This ceremony derives from the life of St Blaise who was Bishop of Sebaste in Armenia. The most popular account of this Saint – *The Acts of St Blaise* – place his martyrdom in the reign of the Emperor Licinius, around 316. Before becoming a bishop, Blaise may have been a physician and it is thought that he, under divine command, fled to the Armenian mountains to escape Licinius' persecution of Christians.

St Blaise lived for some time in caves with wild animals that he blessed and healed as the need arose. He is reputed to have rescued a pig from a wolf's fangs and restored it. For these actions, he is known as one of the patron saints of wild animals.

His most famous healing took place on his way to trial. A child who had swallowed a fish bone was about to die through choking. St Blaise touched the child's throat and dislodged the bone, thus saving the child's life. For centuries after this act, St Blaise has been invoked for every kind of throat ailment. It was common for country priests to remove throat obstructions by holding the sufferer in both hands and saying, 'Blaise, the martyr and servant of Jesus Christ, commands thee to pass up and down'.

Interestingly, because of the manner of his torture before martyrdom (his skin was torn with sharp iron combs), Blaise is also the patron saint of wool combers. His feast day throughout Britain during the nineteenth century was an occasion for great processions involving everyone from the wool trades.

An extract from a report in the *Leeds Mercury* of 5 February 1825 shows the scale of the celebration in Bradford, a major wool industry town:

The different trades began to assemble at eight o'clock in the morning, but it was near ten o'clock before they all were arranged in marching order in Westgate. The arrangements were actively superintended by Matthew Thompson, Esq.

The morning was brilliantly beautiful. As early as seven o'clock, strangers poured into Bradford from the surrounding towns and villages, in such numbers as to line the roads in every direction; and almost all the vehicles within twenty miles were in requisition. Bradford was never before known to be so crowded with strangers. Many thousands of individuals must have come to witness the scene. About ten o'clock the procession was drawn up in the following order:—

Herald bearing a flag.
Woolstaplers on horseback, each horse
caparisoned with a fleece.
Worsted Spinners and Manufacturers on
horseback, in white stuff waistcoats, with
each a sliver over the shoulder, and
a white stuff sash; the horses'
necks covered with nets
made of thick yarn.
Merchants on horseback, with coloured
sashes.
Three Guards, Masters' Colours, Three Guards.
Apprentices and Masters' Sons, on horseback,
with ornamented caps, scarlet stuff
coats, white stuff waistcoats, and
blue pantaloons.
Bradford and *Keighley Bands.*
Mace-bearer, on foot.
Six Guards. KING. QUEEN. Six Guards.
Guards. JASON. PRINCESS MEDEA. Guards.
Bishop's Chaplain.
BISHOP BLAISE.
Shepherd and Shepherdess.
Shepherd Swains.
Woolsorters, on horseback, with ornamented
caps, and various coloured slivers.
Comb Makers.
Charcoal Burners.

Combers' Colours.
Band.
Woolcombers, with wool wigs, &c.
Band.
Dyers, with red cockades, blue aprons, and
crossed slivers of red and blue.

ST JEROME AND THE LION

St Jerome lived during the third century and is one of the four Latin Fathers of the Church. He was born into a wealthy family and is the patron saint of scholars and librarians. A brilliant intellectual, who possessed one of the world's greatest libraries, he lived a pagan life until his baptism around the age of 30.

He diligently studied the life of Christ, but felt his love of non-Christian works would lead him astray. So he became a hermit in Arabia, put on sackcloth, and lived a life of prayer and fasting until he became quite emaciated. His love of learning and desire to know his Saviour led to his studying the Scriptures in Hebrew. Although he struggled with the language, he eventually mastered it and today he is renowned for giving us the first accurate Latin translation of the Bible.

Eventually, he retired to Bethlehem and lived in a monastery that he founded. A lovely story relates that while he was in Bethlehem he saw a lion limping as if in pain. The lion approached him and, while others fled in terror, Jerome took the lion's paw and extracted a thorn. From that time on, the grateful lion refused to leave the saint and Jerome used it to bring him wood from a nearby forest.

The last part of Jerome's life in Bethlehem was full of trouble. From all parts of the Roman Empire news came of the invasion of the barbarians, and in 410 the Goths, under Alaric, sacked Rome itself. Like other countries, the north of Palestine was laid waste, and the monks had to share their scanty food with the crowd that poured into the monasteries for refuge. Tradition holds that St Jerome died in 420 in Bethlehem, with his head resting in the manger where Our Lord was born.

Travellers to Bethlehem are still led through a passage cut in the rock to the cell where Jerome wrote his commentaries, epistles and translations, which have given him a foremost place among students of the Bible.

BOND VILLAINS

The fate of a James Bond villain is nearly always clear cut; by the final scenes, he (for most of them are male) is to die in a gruesome manner. The list of Bond villains and their fate are as follows:

Film	Villain	Fate
Dr No	Dr Julius No	Thrown into a pool of toxic waste by Bond.
From Russia With Love	Rosa Klebb	Killed by Tatiana in the final scene.
Goldfinger	Auric Goldfinger	Sucked out of the cabin of an aeroplane.
Thunderball	Emilio Largo	Speared in the back by Domino.

You Only Live Twice	Ernst Blofeld	Escaped on a mono-rail.
On Her Majesty's Secret Service	Ernst Blofeld	Presumed dead after a car chase.
Diamonds are Forever	Ernst Blofeld	Presumed dead after falling into the ocean.
Live and Let Die	Dr Kananga	Blown up by a pressurized bullet.
The Man with the Golden Gun	Francisco Scaramanga	Shot by Bond.
The Spy Who Loved Me	Karl Stromberg	Shot by Bond.
Moonraker	Hugo Drax	Shot by Bond.
For Your Eyes Only	Aris Kristatos	Shot by Columbo.
Octopussy	Kamal Khan	Flew into a cliff face.
A View to a Kill	Max Zorin	Airship blew up.
The Living Daylights	Georgi Koskov	Arrested and put in prison.
Licence to Kill	Franz Sanchez	Shot by Bond.
Goldeneye	Alec Trevelyan (006)	Impaled on a pole by Bond.
Tomorrow Never Dies	Elliott Carver	Destroyed by his own torpedo.
The World Is Not Enough	Renard	Speared by a nuclear fuel rod.
Die Another Day	Gustav Graves	Chopped up by a jet engine.

IF THOU WILT BE PERFECT . . .

Peter Waldo (1140–1218) was a rich merchant of Lyons, France. One day, he asked a priest how he could live like Jesus Christ. The priest quoted the words of Jesus to the rich young ruler, 'If thou wilt be perfect, go and sell that thou hast, and give it to the poor, and thou shalt have treasure in heaven: and come and follow me' (Matthew 19. 21). Waldo made financial provision for his wife, put his daughters in a convent, and gave the rest of his money to the poor. Waldo memorized portions of the Bible, and began preaching to people. As he gained followers, he sent them out in pairs to preach.

Waldo's followers called themselves 'the Poor in Spirit'. They were also known as the 'Poor of Lyons', the Waldensians (after Waldo), the Wandenses (a variation of Waldensians), and the Vaudois (Vaudes is French for Waldo). The Waldensians were orthodox in their beliefs, but they were outside of the organizational structure of the Roman Catholic Church.

They travelled in pairs, preaching the gospel. They were humble people who believed in 'apostolic poverty'. Travelling barefoot, owning nothing, and sharing all things in common.

The humility and voluntary poverty of the Waldensians were a striking contrast to the pride and luxury of the hierarchy of the Roman Catholic Church. For example, Pope Innocent III (who reigned from 1198 to 1216) wore clothes covered with gold and jewels. He made kings and cardinals kiss his foot. He said that the Pope is 'less than God but more than man'.

Waldo's beliefs were founded on the Bible, especially the Gospels. He believed that there was no need to interpret the Bible because it spoke clearly for itself. All that was needed was to make the whole of Scripture available to the people. Waldo was French, so he commissioned two priests to translate the Bible into French, starting with the Gospels. As soon as the first Gospel had been translated, Waldo applied it to his life 'to the letter' and began preaching it to the people.

Waldo and his followers were excommunicated by Pope Lucius III in 1184 after they refused to stop preaching. Thus began centuries of persecution for a movement that demonstrated the powerful effects of living in accordance with the principles in the Bible. Persecution drove the Waldensians underground in countries such as Italy, Switzerland and Austria. They survived until the sixteenth century, then embraced the Protestant Reformation.

SAINTS AND AMERICAN PLACE NAMES

The history of the United States is reflected in its place names, and there are many saints' names across the 50 American states, including:

County	State	Population	Capital
Saint Bernard	Louisiana	67,229	Chalmette
Saint Charles	Louisiana	48,072	Hahnville
Saint Charles	Missouri	283,883	Saint Charles
Saint Clair	Alabama	64,742	Asheville, Pell City
Saint Clair	Illinois	256,082	Belleville
Saint Clair	Michigan	164,235	Port Huron
Saint Clair	Missouri	9,652	Osceola
Sainte Geneviève	Missouri	17,842	Sainte Geneviève
Saint Francis	Missouri	29,329	Forrest City
Saint Francois	Missouri	55,641	Farmington

Saint Helena	Louisiana	10,525	Greensburg
Saint James	Louisiana	21,216	Convent
Saint Johns	Florida	123,135	Saint Augustine
Saint John the Baptist	Louisiana	43,044	Edgard
Saint Joseph	Indiana	265,559	South Bend
Saint Joseph	Michigan	62,422	Centreville
Saint Landry	Louisiana	87,700	Opelousas
Saint Lawrence	New York	111,931	Canton
Saint Louis	Minnesota	200,528	Duluth
Saint Louis	Missouri	1,016,315	Clayton
Saint Louis	Missouri	348,189	Saint Louis
Saint Lucie	Florida	192,695	Fort Pierce
Saint Martin	Louisiana	48,583	Saint Martinville
Saint Mary	Louisiana	53,500	Franklin
Saint Mary's	Maryland	86,211	Leonardstown
Saint Tammany	Louisiana	191,268	Covington
San Augustine	Texas	8,946	San Augustine
San Benito	California	53,234	Hollister
San Bernardino	California	1,709,434	San Bernardino
San Diego	California	2,813,833	San Diego
San Francisco	California	776,733	San Francisco
San Jacinto	Texas	22,246	Coldspring
San Joaquin	California	563,598	Stockton
San Juan	Colorado	558	Silverton

San Juan	New Mexico	113,801	Aztec
San Juan	Utah	14,413	Monticello
San Juan	Washington	14,077	Friday Harbor
San Luis Obispo	California	246,681	San Luis Obispo
San Mateo	California	707,161	Redwood City
San Miguel	Colorado	6,594	Telluride
San Miguel	New Mexico	30,126	Las Vegas
San Patrico	Texas	67,138	Sinton
San Saba	Texas	6,186	San Saba
Santa Barbara	California	399,347	Santa Barbara
Santa Clara	California	1,682,585	San Jose
Santa Cruz	Arizona	38,381	Nogales
Santa Cruz	California	255,602	Santa Cruz
Santa Fe	New Mexico	129,292	Santa Fe
Santa Rosa	Florida	117,743	Milton

HERESY

One of the primary concerns of early Christianity was that of heresy, generally defined as a departure from traditional Christian beliefs and the creation of new ideas, rituals and forms of worship within the Christian Church. Throughout the ages, Christianity has been buffeted by various heresies, including:

Gnosticism

Followers of this heresy mixed Greek philosophy and Eastern myths with Christianity. They held that God, because he was only good, could not have created a world that contained evil. Therefore, in their view, other forces (or children of God) created our world. One such child was Jesus Christ who came to Earth to share his secret knowledge.

The greatest challenge to traditional Christianity posed by Gnosticism was by Marcion (AD 100–60), who was expelled from the Church for this teaching. After the year 138, his followers formed themselves into a separate body (the Marcionites), though they are also known as the *first Dissenters*. Gnosticism survived long into the Middle Ages, and echoes of it are still to be heard in the teachings of the current-day theosophical movement. (Marcionism survived until about the fifth century AD.)

Montanism

Montanus led this heresy from Phrygia in Turkey in AD 156. The followers of this school of thought were 'zealous, but without knowledge'. For instance, they discouraged marriage, invited martyrdom and set down harsh regimes of fasting. They believed in the imminent end of the world and Christ's immediate return.

When suppression came, the Montanists of Constantinople committed suicide rather than surrender. They gathered in their churches and then set light to them, perishing in the flames.

Monarchianism

This heresy is generally understood to have been responsible for the subsequent rise of another (greater) heresy – Arianism. Followers denied the divinity of Christ, believing him to be an ordinary man who had divine power. For example, Paul of

Samosata, the Bishop of Antioch AD 260–72, preached that Jesus was an ordinary man.

Another branch of this sect disputed the nature of the Trinity.

Arianism

Arius was a priest in Alexandria, who eventually created a storm that would rock the very fundament of Christendom. He protested that his bishop, Alexander of Alexandria, was a monarchian. The subsequent quarrel divided the Church between those who taught that Christ and God were the same and those who taught that God was pre-eminent. Both sides claimed the other as being heretic.

Arius was condemned and excommunicated by a council of over 100 bishops, but another church council threatened to reinstate him. Eventually, Emperor Constantine called on the famous Council of Nicaea – where no less than 300 bishops, together with hundreds of other clergy, were gathered – to decide this problem. Constantine first overruled the Arians, but then changed his mind. So in AD 327 Arius was reinstated and became one of Constantine's advisers.

However, the controversy continued and it required the Eastern Emperor Theodosius to bring together another church council in Constantinople in AD 381. This time the Arians were defeated and the Nicene Creed was officially adopted as the statement of belief for the Christian faith. But it wasn't until the eighth century that Arianism finally disappeared.

Apollinarianism

Apollinaris, Bishop of Laodicea, from about AD 360 began to propagate his idea that Christ had no human soul or spirit, but a divine one. It was an attempt by Apollinaris to reason that Jesus was free of sin, purely divine. This led to a series of edicts by church councils that condemned Apollinarianism as heresy.

Nestorianism

Nestorianus, a monk from Antioch, claimed that Jesus was host to two separate persons – that of the son of God and that of a mortal man. It was, as such, a direct response to Apollinarianism.

Also, Nestorianus, in an attempt to dispel Arianism, disputed the description of 'Mother of God' for Mary – namely because this title indicated that, if Christ was born of her, he had to be younger than her. As he was eternal as God, Mary could only be the mother of Jesus the man.

Scattered remnants of Nestorianism survive today in Iraq, Iran, the United States and South India.

Eutychianism (Monophysitism)

Eutyches was the head of a large monastery near Constantinople and had good contacts at court. His heresy arose as he openly disagreed with the definition of the Christian creed of AD 433 in its condemnation of Nestorianism. He believed that it was a compromise with that heresy, and hence that the Church was guilty of Nestorianism itself.

He claimed that Christ did not possess two natures (divine and human), but that Christ was *of* two natures. In his view, Christ had merged the two natures into one. In AD 451 the great Council of Chalcedon condemned Apollinarianism, Nestorianism and Eutychianism.

Pelagianism

Pelagius, a monk from Britain, gave rise to this heresy. He believed that every child was born absolutely innocent, free of what the traditional Church called 'original sin'. In effect, this meant that Christ was not a saviour who took Adam's original sin upon himself, but merely a teacher who gave mankind an example of what man should be.

Pelagianism is still with us today. Most Christian parents

would struggle to see their new born infant as anything but innocent, and few of them would think they did not possess free will.

SPORTING SAINTS

Team	Sport	Country
New Orleans Saints	American Football	USA
Southampton ('Saints')	Football	England
St Kilda	Aussie Rules Football	Australia
Northampton Saints	Rugby	England
St Helens	Rugby League	England
St Louis Rams	American Football	USA
St Paul Saints	Baseball	USA
St Johnstone	Football	Scotland
St Mirren	Football	Scotland
St Patrick's Athletic	Gaelic football	Eire
St Louis Cardinals	Baseball	USA
St Louis Blues	Ice Hockey	USA

MARY, THE MOTHER OF JESUS

Titles for Mary
Holy Mary,
Holy Mother of God,
Most honoured of virgins,
Chosen daughter of the Father,
Mother of Christ,
Glory of the Holy Spirit
Virgin daughter of Zion,
Virgin poor and humble,
Virgin gentle and obedient,
Handmaid of the Lord,
Mother of the Lord,
Helper of the Redeemed,
Full of grace,
Fountain of beauty,
Model of virtue,
Finest fruit of the redemption,
Perfect disciple of Christ,
Untarnished image of the Church,
Woman transformed,
Woman clothed with the sun,
Woman crowned with stars,
Gentile Lady,
Gracious Lady,
Our Lady,
Joy of Israel,
Splendour of the Church,
Pride of the human race,
Advocate of grace,
Minister of holiness,
Champion of God's people,
Queen of love,
Queen of mercy,
Queen of peace,
Queen of angels,

Queen of patriarchs and prophets,
Queen of apostles and martyrs,
Queen of confessors and virgins,
Queen of all saints,
Queen conceived without original sin,
Queen assumed into heaven,
Queen of all earth,
Queen of heaven,
Queen of the universe

ST BERNARD DOGS

Around AD 1050, an Augustine monastery was founded along the pass between the Swiss Entremont and the Italian Buthier valleys at 2,438 metres (8,000 feet), in memory of St Bernard, a deacon from Aosta in Italy. Bernard was famous for guarding the mountain pass, thus enabling pilgrims to make their way to and from the holy sites in Rome. The area was notorious for thieves and vagabonds and Bernard helped to make it safe.

It was in the sixteenth century that the pass and the monastery were given the name of St Bernard in recognition of their protective duties. Tibetan mastiffs were used for this purpose and the history of the St Bernard dog is linked with development of the monastery as a safe haven for travellers. Dogs at the monastery (and subsquently the famous hospice) did not live to a great age because the humidity of the area led to them suffering from rheumatism.

Records show that by 1750 mountain guides (or *marron-iers*) were routinely accompanied by St Bernard dogs. The dogs' broad chests helped to clear the paths for the travellers. The reports about the dogs' rescue work grew more numerous as it became clear that fatal accidents were decreasing in number. The dogs' primary purpose was to accompany the *marroniers*, as they had an excellent sense of direction. They also possessed an uncanny ability to manoeuvre through heavy fog or snow-storms. The dogs were always accompanied by a monk or *marronier*. However, later on they were allowed on go on rescue missions unaccompanied.

During the 200 or so years that the dogs served on the St Bernard Pass, approximately 2,000 people were rescued. When Napoleon and his army crossed the Alps in May 1800, around 250,000 soldiers travelled through the Pass. The *marroniers* and their dogs were so well organized that, between 1790 and 1810, not one soldier lost his life in the freezing cold of the mountains. The last documented rescue was in 1897 – a 12-year-old boy was found almost frozen to death in a crevice and was awakened by a dog.

The legendary barrel strapped beneath the neck of the dogs, however, seems to have been invented by the famous alpinist Meissner, who wrote in 1816: 'Often the dogs receive a little barrel around their neck with alcoholic beverages and a basket with bread.' The chroniclers from the Hospice never mentioned a barrel. In 1800, however, Canonicus Murith mentioned a little saddle with which the dogs carried milk and butter from the dairy in La Pierre up to the Hospice.

Today, the hospice has 18 St Bernard dogs, but their future is uncertain because instead of these canine helpers of some 60 kilograms, helicopters and heat-seeking equipment are frequently used to rescue people in avalanches.

THE HARP OF THE HOLY SPIRIT

Ephrem (or Ephraim) of Edessa was a teacher, poet, orator, and defender of the faith who died during a famine in AD 373. Edessa was a city in Syria, not far from Antioch – an early centre for the spread of Christian teaching in the East. It is said that in 325 Ephrem accompanied his bishop, James of Nisibis, to the Council of Nicea. His writings are an eloquent defence of the Nicene faith in the deity of Jesus Christ. He countered the Gnostics' practice of spreading their message through popular songs by composing Christian songs and hymns of his own, with great effect. He is known to the Syrian church as 'the harp of the Holy Spirit'. We know of more than 70 of his hymns, numerous Bible commentaries and sermons.

This is one of his well-known poems about fasting, still uttered today in Syria:

O Lord and Master of my life, do not give me the spirit of laziness, meddling, self-importance and idle talk. *[prostration]*

Instead, grace me, Your servant, with the spirit of modesty, humility, patience, and love. *[prostration]*

Indeed, my Lord and King, grant that I may see my own faults,
And not condemn my brothers and sisters, for You are blessed unto ages of ages. Amen. *[prostration]*

[Twelve deep bows, saying each time: 'O God, be gracious to me, a sinner.']

ATHANASIUS OF ALEXANDRIA

Athanasius is revered as a saint by the Roman Catholic and Orthodox denominations, for his outstanding defence of Christianity against the heresy of Arius. Around AD 319, Arius, a church leader, began preaching that Jesus Christ was begotten by God, thus denying the eternality of the Son of God. Athanasius resisted this departure from the Scriptures for most of his life. Although he became Bishop of Alexandria in 318, he was banished at least five times from that city as Arianism took root. It is from his battles with this pernicious heresy that the phrase *Athanasius contra mundum*

(Athanasius against the world) became popular in the fourth century. When he was finally restored to Alexandria, Athanasius formulated a creed that is still recited today to express the unity of the Godhead.

Athanasius was also the first person to identify all 27 books of the New Testament, and his list was accepted by church councils, giving us our New Testament today.

An extract from the Athanasian Creed:

> Whosoever will be saved, before all things it is necessary that he hold the catholic faith;
> Which faith except every one do keep whole and undefiled, without doubt he shall perish everlastingly.
> And the catholic faith is this: That we worship one God in Trinity, and Trinity in Unity;
> Neither confounding the persons nor dividing the substance.
> For there is one person of the Father, another of the Son, and another of the Holy Spirit.
> But the Godhead of the Father, of the Son, and of the Holy Spirit is all one, the glory equal, the majesty coeternal.
> Such as the Father is, such is the Son, and such is the Holy Spirit.
> The Father uncreated, the Son uncreated, and the Holy Spirit uncreated.
> The Father incomprehensible, the Son incomprehensible, and the Holy Spirit incomprehensible.
> The Father eternal, the Son eternal, and the Holy Spirit eternal.
> And yet they are not three eternals but one eternal.

CURIOUS SAINTLY DEEDS
– PART TWO

- St Benno, twelfth-century Bishop of Meissen in Saxony, refused Henry IV (who had been excommunicated) entrance to the Cathedral of Meissen by locking the doors and throwing the key into the River Elbe. He then withdrew to Rome. When he returned to Meissen many months later, he commanded a local fisherman to cast his net into the river. The fisherman brought up a fish with the lost key in its mouth.

- St Cheron, third-century Bishop of Chartres, was on his way to visit St Denis at Paris but was attacked and beheaded by robbers; however, he carried on his journey carrying his head in his hand.

- St Clement is mentioned in Philippians 4.3. He was the third Bishop of Rome and converted many as a result of his miraculous powers. Under the Trajan persecution, Clement was sent with other Christians to work in stone quarries. When they suffered from extreme thirst, Clement prayed and had a vision of Jesus standing near a mountain. Upon digging at this site, a torrent of water was discovered that refreshed them all. Because of this, Clement was thrown into the sea, tied to an anchor. But at the prayer of his brethren, the sea retreated 3 miles.

- St Corentin, the patron saint of Quimper, in Brittany was a fifth-century hermit. Every morning he was sustained by a remarkable fish. Even though Corentin ate a piece of this fish every day, it stayed alive and kept growing. When King Gradlon witnessed this miracle, he had Corentin made the first Bishop of Quimper.

- St Cuthbert was a pupil of St Aidan at Melrose Abbey and later became Bishop of Lindisfarne in the eighth century. He was greatly beloved, and many miracles are attributed to him. On one occasion, he died from long prayers and meditation at the shore, but two otters came out of the water and brought him back to life.

THE LAST SUPPER

Tradition records that in Leonardo da Vinci's masterpiece, 'The Last Supper' the same model was used for the figure of Christ and Judas. The model, Pietro Bandinelli, posed for the portrait of Christ when he was a young chorister in one of Rome's many churches, but for many years da Vinci left the painting unfinished because he could not find the right face to portray Judas. Eventually, he hired a hardened beggar who had hateful features. Da Vinci used him as his model of Judas without realizing he was the same Pietro Bandinelli who years before had looked so much like Christ. The intervening years of sinful living had so marred his countenance that he changed from his Christ-like face to that of the traitor Judas.

RASPUTIN

The last words of Grigory Yefimovich Rasputin, written to Tsarina Alexandra, on 7 December 1916:

I write and leave behind me this letter at St Petersburg. I feel that I shall leave life before January 1st. I wish to make known to the Russian people, to Papa, to the Russian Mother and to the children, to the land of Russia, what they must understand. If I am killed by common assassins, and especially by my brothers the Russian peasants, you, Tsar of Russia, have nothing to fear, remain on your throne and govern, and you, Russian Tsar, will have nothing to fear for your children, they will reign for hundreds of years in Russia. But if I am murdered by nobles, their hands will remain soiled with my blood, for twenty-five years they will not wash their hands from my blood. They will leave Russia. Brothers will kill brothers, and they will kill each other and hate each other, and for twenty-five years there will be no nobles in the country. Tsar of the land of Russia, if you hear the sound of the bell which will tell you that Grigory has been killed, you must know this: if it was your relations who have wrought my death then no one of your family, that is to say, none of your children or relations, will remain alive for more than two years. They will be killed by the Russian people . . . I shall be killed. I am no longer among the living. Pray, pray, be strong, think of your blessed family.

On 30 December, Rasputin was killed by two relatives of the Tsar Nicholas II, and 19 months after Rasputin's death the Tsar and his family were murdered by their Bolshevik guards.

FAMOUS PRISONERS

Prisoner	Prison	For
Al 'Scarface' Capone	Alcatraz	Tax evasion
George 'Machine Gun' Kelly	Alcatraz	Kidnapping
Robert 'Birdman' Stroud	Alcatraz	Murder
William Wallace	Tower of London	Treason
Guy Fawkes	Tower of London	Treason
Sir Walter Raleigh	Tower of London	Treason
Rudolph Hess	Tower of London for four days	Prisoner of war
Anne Boleyn	Tower of London	Treason
Catherine Howard	Tower of London	Treason
Lady Jane Grey	Tower of London	Treason
William Penn	Tower of London	Publication of *The Sandy Foundation Shaken*
Nelson Mandela	Robben Island	Inciting people to go on strike
Winston Churchill	Held by the Boers in 1899	Prisoner of war
Vaclav Havel	Imprisoned three times in Czechoslovakia	Political activities
Fidel Castro	Imprisoned by the Cuban government in 1953	Political activities

Mahatma Gandhi	Imprisoned by the British in 1913	Political activities
Eamon De Valera	Imprisoned by the British in 1916	Easter Rising
Fyodor Dostoyevsky	Four years hard labour in Semipalatinsk	Dissent
John Bunyan	Bedford Jail	Refusal to stop preaching
Daniel Defoe	Newgate	Anti-establish-ment pamphlets
Bertrand Russell	Imprisoned for five months in London in 1918	Libelling the American Army

THE CONVERSION OF A CROOK

 No one is too sinful, too wayward or beyond God's mercy. This wonderful truth is attested to by a brief look at the life of a celebrated sinner who became a powerful instrument of God.

Jerry McAuley was an Irishman who in 1852 was sent to live with his sister in New York, at the age of 13. He lived in the Water Street district of that city and soon became notorious for leading a gang of thugs and thieves. Many times he was in trouble with the law, and by the time he was 19 he had been sentenced to 15 years' imprisonment in Sing Sing Prison.

Five years into his sentence, he went to the Sunday chapel service and heard the testimony of Orville 'Awful' Gardiner. Gardiner had been one of McAuley's crime partners, but he could not deny that a great transformation had taken place in

Gardiner's life. McAuley tried many times to pray for a similar conversion, but struggled to know whether God would forgive him.

Eventually, he found that forgiveness and described that moment thus:

All at once it seemed as if something supernatural was in my room. I was afraid to open my eyes. I was in an agony and the tears rolled off my face in great drops. How I longed for God's mercy! Just then, in the very height of my distress, it seemed as if a hand was laid upon my head and these words came to me: 'My son, thy sins which are many, are forgiven.' I do not know if I heard a voice, yet the words were distinctly spoken in my soul. I jumped from my knees. I paced up and down my cell. A heavenly light seemed to fill it. A softness and a perfume like the fragrance of flowers. I did not know if I was living or not. I clapped my hands and shouted, 'Praise God! Praise God.'

McAuley was released from Sing Sing in 1864 after serving seven years as a result of his reformed life. However, he struggled with being a Christian in the outside world and relapsed several times into crime and drunkenness.

In 1869 McAuley was at the centre of a revival that broke out in the Water Street district. This renewal became known as the John Allen Excitement after the evangelistic preaching of that godly man. McAuley was swept up in this movement and experienced a tremendous spiritual empowering. Fired by the 'Excitement', McAuley and his friend Fredrick Hatch started the 'Helping Hand for Men' mission on 316 Water Street. Night after night they cared for drunks and tramps from the nearby slums. They ministered to thousands of destitute people and preached the gospel to them, as well as taking care of their physical needs.

Although McAuley died in 1884, his influence is still powerful today as there are now hundreds of 'rescue missions', inspired by his example, throughout the United States.

THE 26 MARTYRS OF NAGASAKI

Jesuit missionary Francis Xavier went to Japan in 1549 and succeeded in attracting converts to the Catholic Church. He left after a few years, though, having established several churches and appointed local leaders. Christianity was tolerated in Japan at this time because there was a great interest in developing trading links with the West.

However, the political ruler of Japan (not the Emperor), Toyotomi Hideyoshi, for political reasons began to persecute the few Christians in the country. Believers were arrested, imprisoned and forced to renounce their faith. One of the most notorious incidents took place on 5 February 1597 when 26 men (19 Japanese), among them priests, were forced to march from Osaka to Nagasaki. On the way, their left ears were cut off and they were subjected to cruel tortures. Upon reaching Nagasaki, each man was crucified and then stabbed to death with a spear. None of the men renounced their faith.

As always, this persecution had the opposite effect from what the authorities intended. Instead of snuffing out the faith, the courage of the 26 martyrs inspired other Christians and led to new converts. For a few years, Nagasaki became a major centre of Christianity in the country, as this place of martyrdom was venerated by many pilgrims.

Eventually, in the 1620s, the government expelled all foreigners from Japan. Christianity was absolutely forbidden and contact with the West was broken off, save for a few trading links.

It was not until 250 years later that French priests were allowed back into Japan, and one of their first tasks was to open a church in Nagasaki. They were amazed to discover that native Christians still existed, in spite of the authorities' best attempts to banish them.

Today, there is a monument to the 26 martyrs in Nagasaki at the Martyrs Museum.

FAREWELL, SWEET LIGHT!

St Ambrose, the famed Archbishop of Milan who died in 397, recounts that: 'Theothmus, on being told by his physician that except he did abstain from drink and excess, he was likely to lose his sight. His heart was so desperately set on sin that he said, "Vale lumen amicum: farewell, sweet light! I must have my pleasure in my sin!" '

ANTEPENDIUM

The antependium or *pallium* was the great veil of silk or precious metal that surrounded a saint's altar in the Middle Ages. It was also placed on the tomb itself as a sign of veneration and respect. For example, the basilica of St Ambrosio at Milan preserves an antependium from the ninth century made of gold and covered with precious stones. Where cloth was used, the antependium was often changed with great ceremony.

FOUR CHAPLAINS

On 3 February 1943, the US ship *Dorchester* was torpedoed by a German U boat. On board were four chaplains from the Army Chaplain Corps. Unlike most of the other sailors, the four chaplains had gone to bed with their lifejackets on. When the torpedo hit, many of the sailors could not find their lifejackets in time. In an act of incredible selflessness, the four chaplains gave their own lifejackets to the other sailors, knowing that by doing so they would go down with the sinking ship. Witnesses testified that they last saw the four chaplains with their arms linked together, praying as the ship sank.

This act of courage was recognized with the award of posthumous medals of heroism and a special stamp, issued in 1948. Today, 3 February is designated by the United States Congress as 'Four Chaplains Day'.

The four chaplains were:

- George L. Fox – Methodist minister
- Alexander D. Goode – Rabbi
- Clark V. Poling – Minister of the Dutch Reformed Church
- John P. Washington – Roman Catholic priest

CURIOUS SAINTLY DEEDS – PART THREE

- St Paul the Apostle was beheaded outside the Ostian Gate in Rome around AD 65, the same day as the Apostle Peter was martyred inside the city. Tradition records that as Paul's head was struck off, it bounced three times on the ground. At each place where it touched, a fountain of water sprang up – the first one hot, the second one warm, and the third one cold.

- St Marcarius was one of the most famous Egyptian hermits; he died in the fourth century. Many stories are told about him, including the tale of Marcarius finding the skull of an ancient mummy. He asked the skull who it was and it replied 'a pagan'. When the hermit asked where its soul was, the skull replied, 'Deep in hell!'

- St Isidore is the patron saint of farmers. He was a poor, ignorant peasant whose cruel master did not allow him time for his devotions. However, Isidore continued to pray and worship. His master was converted when he saw the saint deep in prayer and two angels ploughing for him!

- St Herman-Joseph has the latter name because he claimed the Virgin Mary so favoured him that one day she appeared to him in a vision, called him her husband, and put a ring upon his finger.

- St Laurence was from Aragon in Spain and martyred in AD 258 in Rome. He received, from the people of Rome, the title 'Il cotese Spagnuolo' – the Courteous Spaniard. This was because when, 200 years after his death, his tomb was opened to deposit the relics of St Stephen, it was discovered he had moved to the left to accommodate him.

- St Martin of Tours was famed for many miracles. It is said that on one occasion, the Emperor Valentinian came to see him, but failed to show him respect by rising from his chair. However, he quickly got up when the chair suddenly burst into flames.

PLACES LINKED WITH ST PATRICK

The much loved St Patrick came to Ireland in AD 432, on a mission from Pope Celestine I to convert the heathen natives. At that time, Ireland was steeped in Druidism, but Patrick performed many miracles and faithfully presented the Christian faith to the Irish. By the time he died in AD 461, much of the country abandoned Druidism and there was a revival throughout the land.

In Ireland, many places are associated with Patrick, including:

Place	Significance
Lough Derg (Lake of the Red Eye)	An island in County Donegal. It was the last stronghold of the Druids and, according to legend, Patrick slew the monster of the lake here which turned the water red.
Ard Macha	Known today as Armagh. Patrick is reputed to have built the Cathedral Church here.
Ceanannas Mór	Contains the remains of a monastery used by Patrick. Monks from this area created the world-famous *Book of Kells* in the ninth century.
Croagh Phádraig	Upon this mountain in Westport, County Mayo, Patrick spent 40 days fasting and praying.
Sabhail	County Down, allegedly the place where Patrick died.
Dun Phadraig	This fortress in Northern Ireland houses the Cathedral Church of the Holy Trinity, the site of Patrick's burial. St Columba is also supposed to be buried here.

JOHANN TETZEL

Johann Tetzel was a sixteenth-century Dominican priest and master seller of indulgences. Armed with papal authority, he would travel from village to village throughout Germany with printed receipts from the Pope guaranteeing release from purgatory into paradise in exchange for money. Indulgences were popular among the poor, but they were the ones least able to afford them. The money was used to make the Vatican look even grander.

Fraudsters like Tetzel led to Martin Luther posting his famous Ninety-five Theses against papal excesses in Wittenberg on 31 October 1517. Sales of indulgences fell considerably after this.

Tetzel was also accused of immorality and he was disowned by the establishment for his over-enthusiastic sales pitch. He died in 1519. On his deathbed, Luther wrote to him about the forgiveness and salvation offered by Jesus.

One of Tetzel's popular sayings was:

When the coin in the coffer rings, the soul from purgatory springs.

TEN FALSE MESSIAHS

There have been many false messiahs throughout the centuries, claiming divinity and special revelation to restore the greatness of Israel. This is a list of some of these failed deliverers:

Name	What they claimed
Simon Bar Kokhba (132)	Revolted against the Romans and proclaimed himself 'a star, arisen out of Jacob' (Numbers 24.17). Beheaded by the Roman General Julius Severus.
Moses of Crete (450)	Claimed to be a second Moses, but failed to part the Aegean Sea for the people to cross to Israel.

David Alroy (1147)	Skilled magician who revolted against the Sultan of Persia.
Abraham Abulafia (1240–91)	Claimed God had anointed him Messiah in Sicily in 1248. Tried to convert Pope Nicholas III to Judaism!
David Reuveni (1490–1538)	Sought Pope Clement VII's support for a Holy Land crusade. Declared a messiah by Spanish and Portuguese Jews.
Isaac Luria (1534–72)	Claimed he was taught by the prophet Elijah. Developed a new form of Kabbalah. Died at the age of 38 during a flu epidemic.
Hayyim Vital (1542–1620)	A disciple of Luria, and claimed that Luria had made him his successor.
Shabbatai Zevi (1626–76)	Rode to Jerusalem on a white horse, circled the city seven times, and claimed to be able to locate the ten lost tribes. Failed to capture Turkey. Eventually converted to Islam.
Jacob Frank (1726–91)	Expelled from Turkey, converted to Islam, but still claimed messiahship. Died as a result of a stroke.
Rebbe Menechem Mendel Schneerson (1902–94)	Proclaimed as the messiah by the Lubavatcher Chassidic movement in New York. Never visited Israel. Died following a stroke in 1994, but still has a large following.

COLONEL THOMAS BLOOD

Thomas Blood was one of history's most daring criminals. During the English Civil War, he was a spy for Cromwell's forces and was rewarded with land in lieu of wages. After the monarchy was restored, he twice tried to kidnap James Butler, the Lord Lieutenant of Ireland, from Dublin Castle in 1663. Both attempts failed and Blood escaped to Holland dressed as a Quaker!

His most famous criminal activity was an attempt to steal the Crown Jewels from the Tower of London in 1671. Over several months, Blood befriended Talbot Edwards, the Keeper of the Crown Jewels. Eventually, he persuaded Edwards to show him (and his accomplices) the famous Jewels. When Blood and his accomplices were let into the Jewel Chamber, Edwards was quickly bound and gagged. Blood and his gang made off with the Crown Jewels, but somehow Edwards managed to sound the alarm. They were all captured before they left the Tower.

Ironically, Blood and his gang were imprisoned in the Tower. Everyone thought they would hang at Tyburn, but Blood insisted on a meeting with the King. The outcome of that meeting, which took place on 18 July 1671, was that although Blood and his gang were guilty of treason, they were pardoned by the King. In addition, Blood was granted a sum of £500 (a great deal of money at that time) a year for the rest of his life. One explanation for this curious turn of events is that Blood may have served King Charles II as a double agent and his crime was thus overlooked. Another explanation is that he persuaded the King that he wanted to sell the Crown Jewels to bring much needed money into the King's treasury.

Blood died in 1680 in London, but such was his reputation for trickery that his remains were exhumed in 1684 to confirm his identity.

CURIOUS SAINTLY DEEDS
– PART FOUR

- St Thomas of Villanueva was made Archbishop of Valencia in the sixteenth century. He was renowned for his service to the poor and frequently gave away clothes and food to help them. On one occasion, his appearance was so poverty-stricken that his chapter presented him with a large sum of money to buy new clothes. But Thomas gave all the money to the hospital. His great example earned him the title 'Thomas the Almoner'.

- St Etheldreda was an East Anglian Saxon princess in the seventh century. She had a dream that her staff became a great tree. She took this to mean that she must establish a place of religious learning, and so founded Ely Cathedral and monastery, becoming its first abbess. Four hundred years after she died, St Etheldreda is said to have visited and released a repentant sinner who was about to be hanged for his crimes. The man vowed to serve God in the monastery of Ely.

- Clovis, King of the Franks in the sixth century, had a faithful wife, St Clotilda. However, Clovis was not a believer, despite his wife's earnest prayers which seemed to be in vain. But one day on the battlefield Clovis was facing defeat, and called on Clotilda's God and was saved. He emerged victorious from the battle and was baptized by St Remi. At his baptism, tradition holds that a vial of oil came miraculously down from heaven, together with three lilies for Clovis, Clotilda and Remi. Thus the banner of France was changed from three toads to the fleur-de-lys.

- St Ambrose, one of the four Latin fathers of the Church, is the patron saint of Milan. As an infant, a swarm of bees is said to have gathered around his mouth without hurting him, signifying his future eloquence. Many miracles are

attributed to Ambrose. For example, when the Cathedral of Milan was being consecrated, he had a vision that showed him where the relics of St Gervasius and St Protasius were. Once, when he was preaching, he saw an angel encouraging him and he had a vision of the burial of St Martin of Tours taking place in France.

• St Eloy is the patron saint of all metal workers. He was Master of the Mint in Bologna in the seventh century and made many sacred objects for his church. It is said that on many occasions Eloy was tormented by a demon while using his metal-working skills. On one occasion, like St Dunstan, Eloy seized the demon by the nose with his red hot pincers and it fled. Another time, a demon-possessed horse was brought to him that refused to be shod. Eloy cut off the horse's leg, put on the shoe, and replaced the leg by making the sign of the cross.

FIFTH MONARCHY

In Cromwellian England, a Puritan sect known as the Fifth Monarchy Men arose in 1649. They were thus called because they believed they were the successors to the preceding four major monarchies – the Assyrian, the Persian, the Greek and the Roman. They sought to establish a millennial reign of Christ on earth and aimed to abolish all existing laws and the established order. This was to be replaced by Mosaic laws. They had high hopes that Oliver Cromwell would establish such a 'new world order', but they were disappointed when the Protector failed to meet their demands. The Fifth Monarchy Men leaders Christopher Feake and John Rogers were arrested in 1661 and the movement gradually died out – although seeds of it remained for over 100 years.

THE HEAD OF JOHN
THE BAPTIST

On Herod's birthday the daughter of Herodias danced for them and pleased Herod so much that he promised with an oath to give her whatever she asked. Prompted by her mother, she said, 'Give me here on a platter the head of John the Baptist.' The king was distressed, but because of his oaths and his dinner guests, he ordered that her request be granted and had John beheaded in the prison. His head was brought in on a platter and given to the girl, who carried it to her mother.

Mark 14. 6–12

The head of St John the Baptist, the precursor of Christ, has many stories related to it. For instance, the Russian Orthodox Church believes that this famous relic was found and lost at least three times. On the final occasion the head was found (uncorrupted) in 823 in 'the bowels of the earth' where it had been specially hidden by angels. It was transferred from the city of Comana (near the Black Sea) to Constantinople. This find is commemorated by this denomination on 25 May every year as a Third Class Feast.

CURIOUS RUSSIAN SAINTS

- St Andrew became known as the 'Fool for Christ' because he believed he had a calling to act as if insane. He was thrown out of Constantinople and became a beggar. However, his fellow beggars could not stand his behaviour and shunned him. His madness enabled him to pray for those who hurt him and retain his great humility. He is thought to have died in AD 936, aged 66.

- St Herman is reckoned to be the first 'American' Saint of the Russian Orthodox Church. He came to Alaska as a young monk in 1794 and practised an asceticism so severe that no one knew what it was! However, a part of his calling was to carry heavy chains (weighing around 10 kilograms), use two bricks instead of a pillow, and eat very little.

- St Seraphim (Vasyly Nikolaevich Mooraviev), towards the end of his life – in 1940 – prayed for 1,000 days for the salvation of Russia while standing on a rock. It is said that his intercession saved Russia from the Nazis.

- St Agapit was the first recognized medical doctor in Kiev, in the eleventh century. He was also a revered monk who performed many healings, and combined prayers with more conventional techniques such as using herbs. He never accepted payment and was known to have cured many conditions, including leprosy.

COUNT ALESSANDRO DI CAGLIOSTRO

Infamous charlatan, magician and adventurer who enjoyed enormous success in Parisian high society in the years preceding the French Revolution. Born Guiseppe Balsamo in

1743, he took the more impressive-sounding name (and title) Count Alessandro di Cagliostro and travelled throughout Europe posing as an alchemist (selling elixirs of youth and love powders), soothsayer, medium and miraculous healer. By 1785, his séances were gripping Parisian fashionable society.

However, his luck came to an end in 1789 when he was arrested in Rome. His wife had denounced him to the Inquisition as a heretic, magician, conjuror and Freemason. After his trial he was sentenced to death, but this was later commuted to life imprisonment in the fortress of San Leo in the Apennines where he died in 1795.

ST PONTIUS PILATE

Strange but true – Pontius Pilate, fifth governor of Judea from AD 26, is considered a saint, along with his wife Claudia Procula, by the Abyssinian Church. Their tradition holds that Pilate repented of his death sentence upon Jesus after his wife converted him. The acceptance of her Christian faith goes back to the second century; it was believed by no less an authority than Origen. The date of 25 June is assigned to St Pontius and St Procula in the Abyssinian Church and the Greek Church assigns 27 October as a feast day for St Procula.

THE RIGHTEOUS AND THE WICKED COMPARED IN PROVERBS 10

- *Proverbs 10. 3* – The LORD does not let the righteous go hungry, but he thwarts the craving of the wicked.

- *Proverbs 10. 6* – Blessings crown the head of the righteous, but violence overwhelms the mouth of the wicked.

- *Proverbs 10. 7* – The memory of the righteous will be a blessing, but the name of the wicked will rot.

- *Proverbs 10. 8* – The wise in heart accept commands, but a chattering fool comes to ruin.

- *Proverbs 10. 9* – The man of integrity walks securely, but he who takes crooked paths will be found out.

- *Proverbs 10. 11* – The mouth of the righteous is a fountain of life, but violence overwhelms the mouth of the wicked.

- *Proverbs 10. 14* – Wise men store up knowledge, but the mouth of a fool invites ruin.

- *Proverbs 10. 16* – The wages of the righteous bring them life, but the income of the wicked brings them punishment.

- *Proverbs 10. 20* – The tongue of the righteous is choice silver, but the heart of the wicked is of little value.

- *Proverbs 10. 21* – The lips of the righteous nourish many, but fools die for lack of judgment.

- *Proverbs 10. 27* – The fear of the LORD adds length to life, but the years of the wicked are cut short.

- *Proverbs 10. 28* – The prospect of the righteous is joy, but the hopes of the wicked come to nothing.

GOOD KING WENCESLAS

This well-known 'king' was actually the Duke of Bohemia (part of the Czech Republic). Born in 907, Wenceslas's father, Wratislaw, was a Christian but his mother was pagan. He was raised by his grandmother, Ludmilla, who was also a Christian.

Wenceslas became Duke in 922 and sought to christianize the Bohemians. He was keen to introduce the Benedictine Order into his kingdom and was noted for his piety and good works among the poor. Many miracles are associated with Wenceslas. For example, when Radislas, the prince of an invading army, sought to slay him, he saw two angels alongside Wenceslas and heard a heavenly voice warning him not to strike the Duke. He was so astonished at these manifestations that he fell at the feet of Wenceslas and begged his pardon.

It is thought that Wenceslas was murdered by his brother, Boleslas, sometime between 922 and 938. The Duke had provided a banquet at his brother's palace. After the banquet he went to pray, as was his custom, and egged on by his mother, Boleslas struck him down with his sword.

Boleslas was overcome with grief by his actions and had the bones of his brother taken to the church of St Vitus in Prague, where they quickly attracted pilgrims. Within 20 years of his death, he was recognized as the patron saint of Bohemia and his feast day (28 September) is still kept in that land.

The popular carol is thought to have originated in the thirteenth century, although its first recorded appearance was in 1582. The words of today's carol were composed by John Neal, and the music is based on a thirteenth-century spring carol:

Good King Wenceslas looked out
On the feast of Stephen
When the snow lay round about
Deep and crisp and even
Brightly shone the moon that night
Though the frost was cruel
When a poor man came in sight
Gath'ring winter fuel

THE BLOOD OF ST GENNARO

The patron saint of Naples, St Gennaro (or Janarius), is reputed to perform a twice yearly miracle – his dried blood is supposed to liquefy and bubble like fresh blood on at least two days: 19 September and on the Saturday before the first Sunday in May. On these days, the authorities from the Cathedral in Naples display a vial of the saint's liquefied blood to the populace and lead a procession through the city streets.

It is thought that Janarius was martyred during the reign of the Emperor Diocletian in 305. His relics were taken to Pozzuoli, Beneventum and then to Naples. The saint's presence is reputed to have stopped the eruptions of Mount Vesuvius and brought about many healings in the city. Local people believe that if the blood fails to liquefy, disasters such as plague, war and earthquakes are imminent. In 1943, there was great consternation when the blood failed to liquefy.

There have been scientific attempts to explain the phenomenon of blood liquefaction, but so many explanations have been offered that it is difficult to know the truth. In addition, it is claimed that the relics of other saints also manifest blood liquefaction in various degrees, including John the Baptist, Stephen and Pantaleone.

ST POL AND THE DRAGON

In the sixth century, a Welsh prince called Pol became the first Bishop of Leon. He lived in Brittany and had a strange diet that consisted solely of bread and water. He is said to have performed many wonders, including ridding the nearby Isle of Ratz from a terrible dragon by commanding it to cast itself into the sea.

It is said that in Leon Cathedral there still exists Pol's little bell which was found by the saint in the mouth of a fish. This legendary bell is said to cure headaches and similar afflictions by all who listen to it.

THE SIN OF SIMONY

'Disputation with Simon Magus', Fillippino Lippi, 1481.

Simony is the offence of buying or selling for profit something that is spiritual. It is named after Simon Magus, whose story is told in Acts 8. He was a great magician who sought to purchase the power of the Holy Spirit for financial gain.

Now for some time a man named Simon had practised sorcery in the city and amazed all the people of Samaria. He boasted that he was someone great, and all the people, both high and low, gave him their attention and exclaimed, 'This man is the divine power known as the Great Power.' They followed him because he had amazed them for a long time with his magic. But when they believed Philip as he preached the good news of the kingdom of God and the name of Jesus Christ, they were baptized, both men and women. Simon himself believed and was baptised. And he followed Philip everywhere, astonished by the great signs and miracles he saw ... When Simon saw that the Spirit was given at the laying on of the apostles' hands, he offered them money and said, 'Give me also this ability so that everyone on whom I lay my hands may receive the Holy Spirit' (Acts 8. 9–19).

Simony was prohibited by church councils in the third and fourth centuries. But the practice of using money to buy church offices increased and is mentioned as a sin in Dante's *Inferno*, and by Machiavelli, who called, 'luxury, simony and cruelty as three dear friends and handmaids of the Pope'.

The penalty for simony was the forfeiture of any gain from the transaction.

TOUCHING FOR THE KING'S EVIL

That pious monarch, Edward the Confessor (1003–66), began the tradition of 'touching' or laying hands on his subjects to effect a cure for their ailments. According to the *Chronicles of the Kings of England*, a young woman who suffered from 'humours collecting abundantly about her neck, she had contracted a sore disorder, the glands swelling in a dreadful manner' had a  dream to have the affected area washed by the King. When the lady's neck was washed by Edward, 'the lurid skin opened, so that worms flowed out with the purulent matter, and the tumour subsided; but as the orifice of the ulcer was large and unsightly, he commanded her to be supported at the royal expense till she should be perfectly cured. However, before a week was expired, a fair new skin returned, and hid the ulcers so completely that nothing of the original wound could be discovered.' The disease was probably scrofula and was difficult to heal at that time.

The practice of Touching for the King's Evil prevailed with subsequent monarchs and, in 1683, King Charles II regulated this curious ceremony. From that time, 'Publick Healings' were conducted by the King from All Hallows Eve until a week before Christmas and after Christmas until the first week of March. Each person had to be recommended by their minister and issued with a certificate confirming that the individual had an incurable disease and had not previously been touched for the evil.

Many hundreds of cases were recorded of healings being performed by kings from the time of Edward the Confessor onwards, but no records have been uncovered of people who were not cured. It is probable that the psychological impact of the attention of a royal personage did much to assuage the tumours associated with scrofula, but no scientific evidence has been produced to explain this phenomenon completely.

The Touching for the King's Evil is referred to by Shakespeare in *Macbeth*, King Duncan having been a contemporary of Edward the Confessor:

Macduff.—What's the disease he means?
Malcolm.—'Tis called the evil:
A most miraculous work in this good king;
Which often, since my here-remain in England,
I've seen him do. How he solicits heaven,
Himself best knows: but strangely-visited people,
All swoll'n and ulcerous, pitiful to the eye,
The mere despair of surgery, he cures,
Hanging a golden stamp about their necks,
Put on with holy prayers: and 'tis spoken,
To the succeeding royalty he leaves
The healing benediction

Macbeth, *Act 4, Scene 3*

ST DISTAFF'S DAY

The first free day after the Twelve Days of Christmas is 7 January and takes the name of Distaff Day or Rock Dag because, in ancient times, men and women resumed work after the long holiday – the women to their spinning (using a distaff) and the men to ploughing.

It was a day of work and play because it was difficult to resume work after the long break and many pranks were played. Indolent men set fire to the flax of their womenfolk and they doused the men with pails of water! This popular ritual is captured in Robert Herrick's (1591–1674) poem:

St Distaff's Day; Or, the Morrow after Twelfth-day

> Partly work and partly play
> You must on St Distaffs Day:
> From the plough soon free your team;
> Then cane home and fother them:
> If the maids a-spinning go,
> Burn the flax and fire the tow.
> Bring in pails of water then,
> Let the maids bewash the men.
> Give St Distaff' all the right:
> Then bid Christmas sport good night,
> And next morrow every one
> To his own vocation.

THE VICAR OF BRAY

Simon Aleyn was the renowned Vicar of Bray in Berkshire from 1540 to 1588. His notoriety arises from changing his faith to suit the religion of the reigning monarch. He was a Protestant during the reigns of Henry VIII and Edward VI, became a

Catholic during the reign of Mary, and reverted to being a Protestant when Elizabeth I became Queen. His resolve to remain the Vicar of Bray, whatever the circumstances, gave rise to a famous ballad:

The Ballad of the Vicar of Bray

In good King Charles's golden days,
When Loyalty no harm meant;
A Furious High-Church man I was,
And so I gain'd Preferment.
Unto my Flock I daily Preach'd,
Kings are by God appointed,
And Damn'd are those who dare resist,
Or touch the Lord's Anointed.

And this is Law, I will maintain
Unto my Dying Day, Sir.
That whatsoever King may reign,
I will be the Vicar of Bray, Sir!

When Royal James possest the crown,
And popery grew in fashion;
The Penal Law I shouted down,
And read the Declaration:
The Church of Rome I found would fit
Full well my Constitution,
And I had been a Jesuit,
But for the Revolution.

And this is Law, &c.

When William our Deliverer came,
To heal the Nation's Grievance,
I turn'd the Cat in Pan again,
And swore to him Allegiance:
Old Principles I did revoke,
Set conscience at a distance,

[84]

Passive Obedience is a Joke,
A Jest is non-resistance.

And this is Law, &c.

When Royal Ann became our Queen,
Then Church of England's Glory,
Another face of things was seen,
And I became a Tory:
Occasional Conformists base
I Damn'd, and Moderation,
And thought the Church in danger was,
From such Prevarication.

And this is Law, &c.

When George in Pudding time came o'er,
And Moderate Men looked big, Sir,
My Principles I chang'd once more,
And so became a Whig, Sir.
And thus Preferment I procur'd,
From our Faith's great Defender,
And almost every day abjur'd
The Pope, and the Pretender.

And this is Law, &c.

The Illustrious House of Hannover,
And Protestant succession,
To these I lustily will swear,
Whilst they can keep possession:
For in my Faith, and Loyalty,
I never once will faulter,
But George, my lawful king shall be,
Except the Times shou'd alter.
And this is Law, &c.

The British Musical Miscellany, vol. I, 1734, text as
found in R. S. Crane, *A Collection of English Poems
1660–1800*, New York, Harper & Row

THE EARL OF SANDWICH

John Montagu, the fourth Earl of Sandwich, was an eighteenth-century peer who is best remembered for inadvertently inventing the sandwich. The story goes that on one occasion the Earl was so engrossed in a 24-hour gambling session (or it may have been a long working day at the Admiralty) that he sent a waiter to obtain slices of toasted bread and salted beef. To save time, he put the salted beef between two slices of bread and proceeded to eat the first sandwich.

Many scandals overshadowed his political ambitions. For example, he betrayed his one-time friend John Wilkes by reading out Wilkes's pornographic poetry in the House of Lords in order to discredit him.

Montagu was known as 'The Insatiable Earl' for his many excesses. He was a member of the Hell Fire Club, an exclusive collection of 24 aristocrats whose motto was 'Fay ce que voudras' (Do what you will). These rich young men formed themselves into the 'Monks of Medmenham' and conducted mock services in Medmenham in Buckinghamshire. On one occasion, the Earl was trying to summon up the devil and received the fright of his life when one of the members secretly released a baboon into their midst. The Earl thought he had succeeded in his invocation and fled in terror!

The Earl also kept his mistress, Martha Ray, at his estate in Hinchingbrooke House, for over 16 years and had five children with her, despite being married. In 1779, Martha was murdered at Covent Garden by a jealous admirer, Captain Hackman.

The Earl of Sandwich died in 1792 at the age of 74.

SAINTS AND SYMBOLS

Since early times, saints have had symbols associated with them in art to represent their lives and commemorate the manner of their martyrdom. Here are some saints and their symbols:

St Agnes

She was a devoted follower of Jesus who steadfastly refused all offers of marriage, claiming she was the 'bride of Christ'. She is now considered the patroness of chastity. Died AD 654.

St Athanasius

Athanasius was Bishop of Alexandria and a brilliant student of the Holy Scriptures. He was an authority on the ecclesiastical and canon laws of the Church and exerted a powerful influence on the Church. Died AD 373.

St Aidan

An Irish monk who was sent from the monastery on Iona to evangelize northern England; he received the devoted help of Kings Oswald and Oswin. Died AD 651.

St Augustine

Known as the 'Apostle of the English', Augustine and 40 monks brought the gospel to England. He was received by the pagan king, Ethelbert, who was soon baptized along with many others. Later Augustine was made bishop. Died AD 604.

St Alban

He was a pagan who sheltered a persecuted priest, and was then converted. He helped the priest to escape, whereupon the pagans' fury turned on Alban. He was beheaded in the city that now bears his name. Martyred about AD 303.

St Ambrose

This famous Bishop of Milan, one of the four Doctors of the Western Church, was a great lover of music. He added to the richness of sacred services of the Church via music, and introduced the antiphonal chants bearing his name today. Died AD 397.

St Antony of Padua

A faithful and eloquent preacher against doctrinal errors and wickedness, he is usually referred to as the 'hammer of heretics'. A follower of St Francis, he preached in France, Italy and Sicily until his death in Padua. Died AD 1231.

St Cyril of Alexandria

A native of Alexandria and patriarch of the city. Devoted much of his life to the defence of the truth of Christ's divinity. Died AD 444.

St Chrysostom

John, Bishop of Constantinople, became the most eloquent preacher of the early Church, and so was called Chrysostom, meaning 'Golden-mouthed'. Legend says that when he was a baby a swarm of bees settled on his mouth. Died AD 407.

St David

The patron saint of Wales, in which country he was born. He founded many monasteries, the most famous of which was in what is now St Davids. His monks followed a very austere rule. Died about AD 588.

St Columba (St Colum)

This saint founded many churches and monasteries in Ireland and Scotland, the most famous of which was on the island of Iona. One of the most consecrated and indefatigable of Christian missionaries. Died AD 597.

Dunstan

The English-born Dunstan became Abbot of Glastonbury. Legend says that the devil went to Dunstan's cell to tempt him, whereupon Dunstan caught the devil by the nose with red hot pincers and caused him to flee. Died AD 988.

St Gabriel

This archangel was the angel sent to Mary to announce that she was to be the mother of Jesus. He is sometimes called the 'Angel of the Annunciation' (Luke 1).

St George

St George is the patron saint of England and venerated as the model of knight-hood and protector of women. He is also the patron of soldiers as for a long time he was a military man engaged in war-fare with the pagans. Martyred AD 303.

St Katherine (Catherine) of Alexandria

She early converted to Christianity, and vanquished her pagan adversaries in a debate. This so enraged the Emperor that he ordered her to be put to death on a machine of spiked wheels. She was saved by a miracle, but was later beheaded. Martyred AD 310.

St Ignatius

Ignatius was Bishop of Antioch in Syria. When asked by the Emperor for a sacrifice to heathen gods, Ignatius refused. He was condemned and thrown to the wild beasts. Martyred 107 AD.

St Katherine (Catherine) of Siena

From childhood, Katherine was very religious, living at home in extreme self-mortification, and spending much time in prayer and meditation. Later she felt called to leave home and devoted herself to the care of the sick, and other good works. Died AD 1380.

St Michael

One of the archangels, St Michael is regarded traditionally as guardian of the Church and its members against the evil one. It is he who is supposed to weigh the souls of men at the Last Day.

St Lydia

A seller of purple dyes, Lydia was converted through the preaching of St Paul and was baptized, along with her whole household. She was the first recorded Christian convert in Europe (Acts 16. 14). Died in the first century.

St Nicholas

Bishop of Myra. Tradition says that St Nicholas went secretly to the house of a destitute nobleman three nights in succession and threw a purse of gold in the window. Patron saint of children. Died about AD 326.

St Martin

One day Martin saw a shivering beggar and shared his own cloak with this stranger. Later he entered the Church, and while Bishop of Tours he converted his whole area to Christianity. Died AD 401.

St Oswald

First of the English Royal Saints. As King of Northumbria, he diligently sought the complete evangelization of his country, and died fighting against a champion of paganism. Died AD 642.

St Patrick

A captive British boy in Ireland, Patrick escaped and was educated in Continental monasteries. Later he returned to Ireland to preach and teach the gospel and to build churches. Patron saint of Ireland. Died about AD 465.

St Timothy

Companion of Paul on his missionary journeys and referred to by Paul as 'the beloved son in faith'. Reputedly beaten and stoned to death for denouncing the worship of Diana. Died in the first century.

St Raphael

The archangel who is the guardian angel of all humanity. He is called the 'Healer of God' and is identified with the angel of the pool at Bethesda.

St Titus

A convert of St Paul, and mentioned in the Pauline epistles as his brother and co-partner in his labours. Reputedly the first Bishop of Crete. Died in the first century.

St Simeon

As a boy, Simeon joined the community of St John Stylites. For 69 years he lived on the top of pillars within the monastery, in the exercise of religious contemplation. Died about AD 597.

St Valentine

A priest who was active in assisting the martyrs in times of persecution. He was famous for the love and charity that he manifested. Martyred AD 269.

St Stephen

The Deacon and first Christian martyr, called by Luke 'a man full of faith and of the Holy Ghost.' Stoned to death in the first century.

Symbols of the Church, ed. Carroll E. Whittemore, with drawings by William Duncan, Nashville, USA, Abingdon Press, 1957.

PROTECTOR SAINTS

Catholics believe that praying to a particular saint who covers a cause, vocation or medical condition is beneficial. This is a selective list of saints showing the areas they cover. It cannot be a comprehensive list because in many cases more than one saint covers a particular area:

Occupation/Ailment	Saint
Accountants	Matthew
Actors	Genesius
Ague	Petronella
Astronauts	Joseph of Cupertino
Architects	Barbara
Artists	Luke
Authors	Sebastian
Bad dreams	Christopher

Bakers	Elizabeth of Hungary
Bankers	Matthew
Barren women	Antony of Padua
Bachelors	Christopher
Bee keepers	Ambrose
Beggars	Martin of Tours
Blacksmiths	Dunstan
Blind	Lucy
Blood banks	Janarius
Boils	Cosmus
Boy scouts	George
Brides	Nicholas of Myra
Bridegrooms	Nicholas of Myra
Breast cancer	Agatha
Brewers	Armand
Bricklayers	Stephen
Broadcasters	Archangel Gabriel
Butchers	Anthony of Egypt
Cab drivers	Fiacre
Carpenters	Joseph
Children	Agnes
Church	Joseph
Clerics	Gabriel
Cobblers	Bartholomew
Colic	Erasmus
Comedians	Vitus
Computer programmers	Isidore of Seville
Converts	Alban

Cooks	Lawrence
Cowboys	Bernard of Venice
Cripples	Giles
Dancers	Vitus
Death of children	Clotilde
Defilement	Susan
Dentists	Apollonia
Desperate situations	Jude
Dieticians	Martha
Doctors	Pantaleon
Dog bites	Vitus
Doubts	Catherine
Ecologists	Francis of Assisi
Epilepsy	Valentine
Fire fighters	Florian
Fishermen	Andrew
Funeral directors	Joseph of Arimathea
Gardeners	Fiacre
Girl Guides	Joan of Arc
Goldsmiths	Anastasius
Gout	Wolfgang
Grocers	Michael
Headaches	Theresa of Avila
Healers	Brigid of Ireland
Heart patients	John of God
Hopeless cases	Jude
Hospital administrators	Basil the Great
Hunters	Eustachius

Idiocy	Gildas
Infamy	Susan
Invalids	Roch
Jewellers	Eligius
Lawyers	Thomas More
Learning	Ambrose
Leprosy	Lazarus
Librarians	Jerome
Lost items	Antony of Padua
Lovers	Valentine
Married women	Monica
Mentally ill	Dympna
Messengers	Gabriel
Motorists	Anthony the Great
Musicians	Cecelia
Newlyweds	Dorothy
Nurses	Agatha
Orators	John Chrysostom
Palsy	Cornelius
Pawnbrokers	Nicholas
Philosophers	Justin
Physicians	Luke
Plague	Roch
Plasterers	Bartholomew
Poets	David
Police officers	Michael
Printers	John of God
Prisoners	Dismas

Quenching fire	Florian
Quinsy	Blaise
Radiologists	Michael
Rheumatism	James the Greater
Sailors	Brendan
Scabs	Rooke
Scientists	Albert the Great
Sculptors	Claude
Servants	Martha
Skaters	Lidwina
Skiers	Bernard
Skin diseases	Marculf
Sleepwalking	Dymphna
Smallpox	Martin of Tours
Soldiers	Martin of Tours
Sore eyes	Augustine of Hippo
Spinsters	Andrew
Storms	Barbara
Students	Thomas Aquinas
Sudden death	Martin of Tours
Sudden death	Barbara
Tailors	Homobonus
Television	Clare of Assisi
Theologians	Augustine
Throat ailments	Blaise
Toothache	Appolonia
Travellers	Christopher
Troubled families	Eustace

Unhappy husbands	Gomer
Unhappy wives	Uncumber
Venereal disease sufferers	Fiacre
Vermin	Huldrick
Victims of betrayal	Oswin
Victims of unfaithfulness	Catherine of Genoa
Widows	Frances of Rome
Widowers	Edgar
Wool combers	Blaise
Women in labour	Anne
Wealth	Anne

CHANG SHEN

Chinese evangelist Chang Shen (Blind Chang) lived in the Manchuria region of China in the late nineteenth century. Before his conversion to Christianity, Chang was a notorious thief, gambler and womanizer. Local villagers called him Wu So Pu Wei Te (Not an ounce of good), and when he was struck blind, neighbours reckoned it was a judgement from God.

When Chang heard of a missionary hospital hundreds of miles away where people were having their sight restored, he undertook an arduous journey lasting many days to see if they could help him. Unfortunately, all the hospital beds were taken, but the hospital chaplain gave Chang his own bed. There, Chang's physical and spiritual sight was restored as he received medical treatment and a Christian baptism.

Chang spread the gospel to his whole village upon his return, winning hundreds of converts. He committed most of the New Testament to memory, a necessary feat as his sight once again deteriorated.

During the early months of 1900, most of China rose up

against foreign 'devils' in a series of Boxer rebellions. When the Boxers reached Chang's village, they threatened to kill 50 people unless he was handed over to them. Chang was ready to embrace martyrdom and refused all attempts by his captors to worship Buddha.

No one knows when Chang died, but it is reported that as the Boxer leaders led him through the city walls to his death, he sang a hymn that he had learned at the mission hospital many years before that included these lines:

Jesus loves me, He who died Heaven's gate to open wide;
He will wash away my sin, Let His little child come in.
Jesus loves me, He will stay, Close beside me all the way;
If I love Him when I die, He will take me home on high.

ST ANGELA OF FOLIGNO

This saint is a great example of the power of repentance. Angela was born around 1284 and lived in the village of Foligno, about 10 miles from Assisi in Italy. She was a wealthy pagan who married young and had several children. She also lived a scandalous life and committed adultery with several lovers, producing yet more children.

However, in her thirties, her husband died and she experienced a moral crisis. She felt her sins were so great that she could not confess them such was her shame. So she prayed to St Francis of Assisi, who had died about 50 years before. He is said to have appeared to Angela in a dream, promising to help her.

Shortly after this, she met a Franciscan friar and she felt able to make a full confession to him. She underwent a conversion, did penance for her sins, and committed her life to the

Franciscan order. She made a pilgrimage to Rome, sold all her worldly goods, and became a Franciscan lay person.

Her new life led to many visionary experiences that are recorded in her writings – *Memoriale* and *Instructiones* – which she wrote for her sons and others who could learn from her experience. It is thought that she was endowed with the stigmata.

Today, Angela is invoked for many causes, including widows, the death of children, people ridiculed for their piety, and those suffering from sexual temptation. Curiously, she is also known as the 'Mistress of Theologians'.

He [Christ] told me, 'Those of my little children who withdraw from my kingdom by their sinning and make themselves sons of the devil, when they return to the Father, because he rejoices over their return, he demonstrates to them how especially joyful he is. Such indeed is his joy that he grants them a special grace that he does not grant to others who were virgins and had never gone away from him.

Extract from Memoriale

CHRISTIAN PIONEERS IN SCIENCE

The twentieth century saw the worlds of faith and science move further and further apart. However, many pioneers of science were also faithful men who saw in scientific developments many opportunities to testify to the glory of God. The hall of fame includes:

Name	Known for
Sir Francis Bacon (1561–1626)	Father of inductive reasoning

Johann Kepler (1571–1630)	Founder of physical astronomy
Robert Boyle (1627–1691)	Father of modern chemistry
Blaise Pascal (1623–1662)	Mathematician
John Ray (1627–1705)	Father of English natural history
Nicolaus Steno (1631–1686)	Founder of stratigraphy
William Petty (1623–1687)	Founder of statistics
Isaac Newton (1642–1727)	Discovered the law of gravity and inventor of the cat flap
Benjamin Franklin (1706–1790)	Invented the lightning rod
Carolus Linnaeus (1707–1778)	Founder of biological taxonomy
Johann Carl Friedrich Gauss	Discoverer of the law of quadratic reciprocity
Michael Faraday (1791–1867)	Inventor of the electrical generator
Charles Babbage (1792–1871)	Founder of computer science
John Dalton (1766–1844)	Invented atomic theory
Matthew Maury (1806–1873)	Father of oceanography
James Simpson (1811–1879)	Discovered chloroform
James Joule (1818–1889)	Father of thermo-dynamics
Gregory Mendel (1822–1884)	Father of genetics
Louis Pasteur (1822–1895	Father of bacteriology
Joseph Lister (1827–1912)	Founder of antiseptic surgery

Georg Cantor (1845–1918)	Discoverer of the theory of infinite sets
Thomas Edison (1847–1931)	Inventor of over 1,000 devices, including the phonograph and the light bulb
William Mitchell Ramsay (1851–1939)	Archaeologist
Georges Lemaître (1894–1966)	Formulated the Big Bang theory

HOLOCAUST HEROES

The story of Oscar Schindler has become well known through the Steven Spielberg film, *Schindler's List* (itself based on the 1982 book *Schindler's Ark* by Thomas Keneally). Schindler outwitted the Gestapo and saved more than 1,200 Jews from the Nazi death camps. It is heartening to know that Schindler's heroism was echoed by many others who defied Nazi attempts to exterminate the Jews. These Holocaust heroes include:

- Raoul Wallenberg, a Swedish diplomat based in Budapest in 1944–5. In defiance of Nazi rules, he issued 30,000 Jews with passes that enabled them to escape the Gestapo.

- Per Anger, another Swedish diplomat based in Budapest. He worked with Wallenberg to assist thousands of Jews to flee Hungary.

- Frederich Born, a Swiss national who saved over 12,000 Jews in Budapest by issuing them with Red Cross documents.

- Aristides de Sousa Mendes, a French diplomat based in

Bordeaux. Issued 30,000 passes to Jews, allowing them to escape to Portugal.

- Georg Ferdinand Duckwitz, a German diplomat based in Copenhagen. Risked his life by warning the Danish government of plans to deport Danish Jews. He is credited with saving over 7,000 Jews.

- Chiune Sugihara, a Japanese diplomat based in Lithuania. Issued hundreds of Jews with Japanese visas and saved over 1,000 people through his actions.

- Varian Fry, an American journalist. He established the American Relief Centre in Nazi France and rescued hundreds of refugees.

- Nicholas Winton, also known as the 'British Schindler'. He rescued 669 Czechs with help from the British Embassy in Prague. He was knighted in 2002.

SAINTLY OIL

It is said that some saints' relics have an oily substance flowing from them. The origin of this 'oil' is uncertain; it could be from lamps around the shrines of relics or from the relics themselves. The oil from the relics of St Martin of Tours and St Nicholas of Myra is said to have miraculous healing properties and was much sought after in the Middle Ages.

The saintly oil of St Walburga in Eichstadt in Bavaria, which is thought to be mostly water, has been used as a remedy against many diseases.

The oil of St Menas of Baumma in Libya made it a famous place of pilgrimage in the sixth century.

The tomb of St John the Evangelist was supposed to issue an oily substance in the seventh century. Similarly, the tomb of the Apostle Andrew was said to issue fragrant oil.

Other saints who are associated with this phenomenon include:

- St John the Almsgiver, Patriarch of Alexandria, d. 620 or 616.
- St John of Beverley, Bishop of York, d. 721.
- St Luke the Younger, a Greek hermit, d. 945–6.
- St Paul, Bishop of Verdun, d. 648.
- St Perpetuus, Bishop of Tongres-Utrecht, d. 630.
- St Reverianus, Bishop of Autun, and Companions, martyred about 273.
- St Sabinus, Bishop of Canosa, d. about 566.
- St Sigolena, Abbess of Troclar, d. about 700.
- St William, Archbishop of York, d. 1154.

ST MAMMERTUS AND ROGATION DAYS

St Mammertus was Archbishop of Vienne in Dauphine, France, in the fifth century. A learned scholar, he is chiefly remembered for reviving the series of fasts and prayers called 'Rogations' during the three days before the feast of the Ascension of Our Lord. Rogation comes from the Latin *rogatio* or *rogare*, meaning to beseech.

The idea of reviving Rogations came about in this way. The city of Vienne had been ravaged by wars, fires and earthquakes, and some considered these to be a divine judgement arising from the lax morals of the people. In the midst of these terrors, Mammertus prayed and received assurance of divine mercy. A terrible fire that was raging through Vienne suddenly ceased and the local people attributed this to a miracle resulting from Mammertus' prayers.

Mammertus decided that the practice of Rogations should be recommenced as a thanksgiving to God. In 475, the Church of Auvergne was used for this purpose, and very soon churches throughout the country had Rogation services. Pope Leo III recognized the importance of Rogation services shortly after, and today Rogation Sunday is still part of the church calendar. In some churches, the ancient date for Rogation Day (25 April) is still kept and referred to as Major Rogation Day, with the three days before Ascension known as Minor Rogation Days.

In the Middle Ages, it was common to perform the ceremony of 'beating the bounds' during Rogation Week. This was a formal procession of boys around the parish boundary, led by the parish priest. At the boundary points and other notable landmarks, scriptures were read, prayers were offered, and the boys were knocked against the boundary stones to make sure they remembered the parish limits! Elements of this ancient ceremony are still performed in many parishes today.

KING MANASSEH

King Manasseh was the thirteenth King of Judah and reigned in Israel for 55 years from 722 BC. His story is found in 2 Kings 21. 1–17 and 2 Chronicles 33. 1–20. Although Manasseh's father, Hezekiah, was a godly man, Manasseh is the most notorious of the Kings of Judah because of his evil acts, including:

- Sacrificing his children to heathen deities.
- Placing an idol in the temple.
- Getting rid of the Ark of the Covenant.
- Rebuilding pagan shrines.
- Murdering so many people that the streets of Jerusalem ran with blood.
- Leading his people astray 'so that they did more evil than the nations the LORD had destroyed before the Israelites' (2 Chronicles 33. 9).

This wicked man was eventually imprisoned by the Assyrians who humiliated him by taking him into exile. In his distress, Manasseh confessed his sins and turned to the Lord. Amazingly, he was restored to his throne where he set about undoing all his evil ways. He destroyed the pagan shrines, removed his idols from the temple, and restored temple worship. However, Judah still had to face the consequences of Manasseh's reign and the subsequent fall of the kingdom is blamed on Manasseh.

The story of Manasseh affords a wonderful lesson about God's mercy. Even a thoroughly wicked man like Manasseh was heard by God because of his humility and earnest repentance. Manasseh's life shows that no one is wholly excluded from God's provision and, whatever our past deeds, God is looking to forgive us and restore us as we acknowledge his ways:

> Manasseh was twelve years old when he became king, and he reigned in Jerusalem for fifty-five years. He did evil in the eyes of the LORD, following the detestable practices of the nations the LORD had driven out before the Israelites. He rebuilt the high places his father Hezekiah had demolished; he also erected altars to the Baals and made Asherah poles. He bowed down to all the starry hosts and worshipped them. He built altars in the temple of the LORD, of which the LORD had said, 'My Name will remain in Jerusalem for ever.' In both courts of the temple of the LORD, he built altars to all the starry hosts. He sacrificed his sons in the fire in the Valley of Ben Hinnom, practised sorcery, divination and witchcraft, and consulted mediums and spiritists. He did much evil in the eyes of the LORD, provoking him to anger (2 Chronicles 33. 1–6).

> In his distress he sought the favour of the LORD his God and humbled himself greatly before the God of his fathers. And when he prayed to him, the LORD was moved by his entreaty and listened to his plea; so he brought him back to Jerusalem and to his kingdom. Then Manasseh knew that the LORD is God (2 Chronicles 33. 12–13).

FAMOUS RELICS

According to the legend, when the Emperor Charlemagne had finished building the church of Our Lady in Aix-la-Chapelle, France, he set himself the task of collecting famous relics from Rome, Constantinople, Jerusalem and other centres of Christendom.

Among the relics he managed to obtain were:

- The tunic of the Blessed Virgin.
- The swaddling-clothes of the infant Jesus.
- The loincloth worn by Jesus on the cross.
- The cloth in which the head of St John the Baptist was enveloped after his decapitation.
- A small piece of the cord with which Christ was bound during the flagellation.
- The girdle of the Virgin.
- A bit of the sponge that was offered to Christ on the cross.
- A lock of hair from the head of St Bartholomew.
- Two of St Thomas the Apostle's teeth.
- One of the arms of the old Simeon.
- A fragment of the cross.
- A tooth of St Catherine.
- The point of a nail with which Christ was attached to the cross.
- A bit of the rod that served in the mocking of Christ.
- A lock of hair from the head of St John the Baptist.

These relics were exhibited every seven years during the period 10 to 24 July and drew enormous crowds.

The tunic of the Virgin was said to be yellowish in colour, 5½ feet in length, and 3¼ feet in circumference, with a small amount of decoration. The swaddling-clothes of the infant Jesus were folded three times in double folds and had brownish yellow ribbons. The blood-stained linen of St John the Baptist was of fine texture, folded and bound with red ribbons. The linen cloth that was bound round Christ's loins upon the cross was of a heavy texture, folded, and was very blood-stained. It was folded in a triangular shape, 4 feet 2½ inches in length, and 4 feet 10 inches in width.

ST VALENTINE

Little is known about this celebrated saint, but it is thought he was a fourth-century Roman who was martyred during the reign of Claudius II. His feast day, on 14 February, supersedes the ancient Roman festival of Lupercalia when young men and women drew lots for one another.

Valentine is the saint of lovers, and in former times it was the custom for men to send presents to their sweethearts. In some places, it was the tradition that the gentleman's valentine was the first lady he saw on Valentine's Day – and vice versa for ladies.

In England in the eighteenth century, the eve of St Valentine's Day was celebrated thus: an equal number of maids and bachelors came together, with each writing their true love's name, and a feigned name, upon separate tickets. These were rolled up and lots were drawn, so that each girl was randomly matched to each lad, and each lad matched to each girl. By this means, everyone had two partners, but the lad had to select the valentine. The couples then spent the next few days feasting and dancing.

Many songs, poems and ballads were sung on St Valentine's Day, including this invocation to the saint:

> Hast, friendly Saint! to my relief,
> My heart is stol'n, help! stop the thief!
> My rifled breast I search'd with care,
> And found Eliza lurking there.
> Away she started from my view,
> Yet may be caught, if thou pursue;
> Nor need I to describe her strive –

The fairest, dearest maid alive!
Seize her – yet treat the nymph divine
　　With gentle usage, Valentine!
Then, tell her, she, for what was done,
Must bring my heart, and give her own.

Samuel Pepys noted Valentine's Day 1667 thus: 'This morning came up to my wife's bedside (I being up dressing myself) little Will Mercer to be her valentine, and brought her name written upon blue paper in gold letters, done by himself, very pretty; and we were both well pleased with it. But I am also this year my wife's valentine, and it will cost me £5: but that I must have laid out if we had not been valentines.'

ST PAUL THE SIMPLE

This saint is thus called because he did not have of the gifts of intellect or high learning. He lived in the second century as a hermit in Egypt, but his calling came at great cost.

It is said that he journeyed for eight days into the desert to become a disciple of St Antony. But Antony would not accept him, and told him to return home. However, Paul fasted, prayed and waited at Antony's door until he was admitted. In order to test Paul's commitment, Antony put many trials in his way, including:

- Asking him to undo his diligent work of making mats and begin all over again.
- Spilling honey in the desert sand and asking Paul to gather it up without any grain of sand in it.
- Ordering him to sew and unsew garments.
- Go seven days without eating.

Even after he proved himself through these trials, Paul was only allowed a cell some 3 miles distant from Antony. It is said that Paul cured many sick and demon-possessed people in the desert. He died around 330.

SOLSTICE SAINTS

Before the advent of artificial light dulled our sense of the importance of seasons, the two solstices marked key turning points in the year. The winter solstice occurs in dark days in the Northern Hemisphere, when all of nature seems static. The summer solstice promises warmth and light, but with the knowledge that the sun has already reached its greatest strength.

In ancient times, the festivals of saints around the time of the winter and summer solstice were particularly important as they gave the opportunity to replace pagan traditions with Christian customs.

There are three main solstice saints, these being:

- St Lucy (meaning light), whose feast day on 13 December marked the winter solstice in the old calendar. The customary rhyme, 'Lucy-light, shortest day and longest night', connects the saint to the winter solstice. Lucy is honoured as a virgin martyr who refused marriage to a pagan and was killed in 304. She is the patron saint of all who have eye diseases, because she was supposed to have been blinded by her tormentors. Swedish people call Lucy's Day 'Little Yule' because it falls near the season of Advent. On Lucy's Day, most Swedish rural households used to choose the youngest girl to be the Lucia Queen. She had to rise early and wake everyone up with her special song and then hand out gifts of food. In many parts of Europe, St Lucy was sometimes the companion of St Nicholas as the bringer of gifts.

- Thomas the Apostle (Doubting Thomas) has his feast day

on 21 December. Because of his doubting nature, in many parts of Europe Thomas was represented as a mysterious figure of light and dark. He is invoked for protection against witches, but also associated with calling the dead to rise from their graves. St Thomas's Day was greatly celebrated in schools because it was the custom to lock the doors to shut the schoolteachers out! Instead of lessons, the children took to play and sang, as for example in rural Scotland: 'This is the shortest day, an' we maun hae the play; an' if ye wunna gies the play, we'll steek ye oot a the day!'

- John the Baptist is the saint of the summer solstice, his feast day being Midsummer Day, 24 June. Bonfires were lit in his honour across the hilltops in many European countries, and there used to be grand parades to commemorate his life. It was thought that a barren woman who walked naked in her garden at midnight to gather St John's Wort would conceive within a year. John the Baptist is the patron saint of bird dealers, epileptics, farriers, lambs and motorways.

ST ELIZABETH ANN SETON

Elizabeth Ann Seton is known as the first American-born saint. She was beatified in 1963 and canonized in 1975 for her work in founding the Sisters of Charity Mission in America – the first religious community for women in that nation.

She was born into a committed Episcopalian family in 1774 in New York, but lost her mother and a younger sister while still a child – a fate she bore with customary courage and steadfast hope.

She married a wealthy businessman, William Magee Seton, at 19 and had five children. However, he died of tuberculosis while visiting Italy and she was reduced to living the life of a penniless widow with five children to support. Elizabeth adopted the Catholic faith in March 1805, after visiting Italy with her husband.

Although poor, in partnership with her sister-in-law, Rebecca, Elizabeth founded the Society for the Relief of Poor Widows with Small Children. With help from her friends, she also opened a boarding school for boys (St Joseph's Academy and Free School) and then a similar school for girls. These institutions were run along the lines of a religious order and eventually became a community of nuns.

The order of nuns grew and quickly expanded in other areas to serve as hospitals, orphanages and schools. Elizabeth died in 1821 and is buried in Emmitsburg, Maryland. She is remembered on 4 January in the calendar of saints.

What stands out about Elizabeth Ann Seton is her ordinariness – she was not a mystic or stigmatic. She had no great spiritual gifts, but accomplished much because she abandoned herself to God, as is made clear by one of her most famous quotes: 'The first end I propose in our daily work is to do the will of God; secondly, to do it in the manner he wills it; and thirdly, to do it because it is his will.'

MEXICAN MARTYRS

After years of civil war and revolutionary struggle, the year 1917 witnessed a new Mexican constitution initiated by President Venustiano Carranza. Although in theory this gave freedom of expression to all faiths, the years that followed were a period of intense religious persecution because of the chaotic state of the country, characterized by tribal violence, rampant inflation, food shortages and poor communications.

The nationalistic government expelled foreign priests, a move that led to the formation of a guerrilla organization called the 'Cristero Movement'. It was during these years of struggle that many priests were murdered, including the following 25 martyrs:

Name	Date
Fr Cristóbal Magallanes Jara	Shot on 25 May 1927
Fr Agustín Caloca Cortés	Shot on 25 May 1927
Fr José Maria Robles Hurtado	Hanged on 26 June 1927
Fr David Galván Bermúdez	Shot on 30 January 1915
Fr Justino Orona Madrigal	Shot on 1 July 1928
Fr Atilano Cruz Alvarado	Shot on 1 July 1928
Fr Román Adame Rosales	Shot on 21 April 1927
Fr Julio Álvarez Mendoza	Shot on 30 March 1927
Fr Pedro Esqueda Ramírez	Shot on 22 November 1927
Fr Rodrigo Aguilar Alemán	Hanged on 28 October 1927
Fr Tranquilino Ubiarco Robles	Hanged on 5 October 1928
Fr Jenaro Sánchez Delgadillo	Hanged on 17 January 1927
Fr José Isabel Flores Varela	Beheaded on 21 June 1927
Fr Sabás Reyes Salazar	Shot on 13 April 1927
Fr Toribio Romo González	Shot on 25 February 1928
Fr Luis Batiz	Shot on 15 August 1926
Manuel Morales	Shot on 15 August 1926
Salvador Lara Puente	Shot on 15 August 1926
David Roldán Lara	Shot on 15 August 1926
Fr Mateo Correa Magallanes	Shot on 6 February 1927
Fr Pedro de Jesús Maldonado	Shot on 11 February 1937

Fr Jesús Méndez Montoya	Shot on 5 February 1928
Fr David Uribe Velasco	Shot on 12 April 1927
Fr Margarito Flores García	Shot on 12 November 1927
Fr Miguel de la Mora	Shot on 7 August 1927

On 22 November 1992 these martyrs were beatified and on 21 May 2000 they were canonized by Pope John Paul II. Today, over 95 per cent of the population in Mexico classifies itself as Christian.

> Be faithful, even to the point of death, and I will give you the crown of life.
>
> *Revelation 2. 10*

ST MONICA – LAPSED CATHOLICS

St Monica (331–88) is known as the patron saint of lapsed Catholics and unfaithful husbands. More famously, she is the mother of Augustine the Great, Bishop of Hippo. However, her brilliant son was very self-willed and for 12 years left the Catholic faith and joined a heretical sect called the Manichees, where he lived an immoral life and refused to be baptized. During this time, she also had to contend with her husband, Patricius, who was a bad-tempered pagan given to having affairs with other women.

She was so angry with Augustine that she kicked him out of the house and pleaded every day with God for his return to the Catholic faith. She did not nag Patricius, but let him see – by the example of her life – how true happiness can be experienced. A year before his death, Patricius was converted.

When Augustine left for Rome to become a teacher of rhetoric, Monica continued faithfully in prayer for him and eventually joined him in Milan. There her prayers were answered, when Augustine abandoned the Manichees and accepted the Catholic faith in 386. Her words to Augustine upon his turning to the Catholic faith, a few days before she died, are recorded in *Augustine's Confessions*: 'Now my hopes in this world are accomplished. One thing there was for which I desired to linger for a while in this life, that I might see thee a Catholic Christian before I died. My God hath done this for me more abundantly, that I should now see thee withal despising earthly happiness.'

SHE WHO MOVES FORWARD

Kateri Tekakwitha is the first native American to become a saint. She was a born into the Turtle Clan of the Iroquois tribe in 1656 along the south bank of the Mohawk River near a village called Ossernenon. It is thought that her mother was a Christian and her name, Tekakwitha, means 'she who moves forward', or 'she who puts things in order'.

Before her fifth birthday, Kateri survived a smallpox epidemic that claimed the lives of her parents and baby brother. But the disease impaired her vision and scarred her face. Following the death of her parents, she was raised by tribal parents.

In 1667 the area was visited by Jesuit missionaries (known as the Blackrobes) and she came to a knowledge of the Christian faith through this contact. The Blackrobes established a mission nearby and, despite tribal opposition, she was baptized on 5 April 1676, taking the name Kateri (Indian for Catherine).

She suffered persecution from her tribe and eventually had to flee the encampment, with the help of other Christian Indians. She remained a steadfast Christian despite much opposition and died on 17 April 1680 at the age of 24.

The case for her canonization was started in 1884 under Pope Leo XIII and she was beatified by Pope John Paul II on 22 June 1980. She is recognized as the patron saint of ecologists, exiles, orphans and people ridiculed for their faith.

YOU DON'T HAVE TO BE A ROCKET SCIENTIST TO BE THE PATRON SAINT OF ASTRONAUTS

Joseph Desa, who became St Joseph of Cupertino, patron saint of astronauts, had nothing to commend him as a child. This Franciscan friar, born on 17 June 1603 near Brindisi, Italy, was also known as Joseph the Dunce.

As a child, he received ecstatic visions but did not know what to make of them. He was useless at school, absent minded, awkward, a poor speaker and nervous. He was not wanted as a child and his slowness made him more and more isolated at home.

Without any hope of a vocation, he tried to become a monk and was initially refused because of his lack of education. When he was accepted as a lay brother in 1620, the monks found they could not do anything with him because of his ecstatic visions, which rendered him insensible. When he received a vision, it was as if Joseph turned to stone and the monks had to prick him with needles to enable him to return to the real world.

He could barely read or write, but his devotion to Christ led to a series of extraordinary visions and miraculous healings. It is said that he would often levitate (hence the connection to astronauts) while experiencing these visions and had a deep understanding of the mysteries of faith. He seemed to have a discerning heart and was able to communicate with animals in much the same way as Francis of Assisi. Moreover, despite his disadvantages he was a cheerful soul, often caught up in the experience of God.

However, because of the controversy surrounding his ecstasies, he was not allowed to be in the choir or eat with the other monks and was placed in his own cell so that he didn't embarrass the other monks. He was even questioned by the Spanish Inquisition, but did not allow their threats to take away his joyous spirit.

He died on 18 September 1663 and was canonized in 1767 by Pope Clement XIII. His life exemplifies the sovereign choice of God, as found in 1 Corinthians:

> But God chose the foolish things of the world to shame the wise; God chose the weak things of the world to shame the strong. He chose the lowly things of this world and the despised things – and the things that are not – to nullify the things that are, so that no one may boast before him.

> *1 Corinthians 1. 27–9*

A MODERN RELIC CERTIFICATE

Although most relics belong to the Middle Ages, they are still widely used as objects of devotion in the Roman Catholic and Orthodox Churches. It is still possible to obtain a relic (from a 'relic bank' in Rome), although it is forbidden under church law to charge for a relic (apart from a charge for the required relic case). In most cases, the relic provided is a very small piece of bone or skin, accompanied by a certificate of authenticity signed by the Keeper of Relics. The example

below is a relatively modern certificate for relics from St
Valentine sent from Rome to Dublin.

Translation of letter accompanying the remains of
St Valentine:

St Valentine

We, Charles, by the divine mercy, Bishop of Sabina of the
Holy Roman Church, Cardinal Odescalchi arch priest of the
sacred Liberian Basilica, Vicar General of our most Holy
Father the Pope and Judge in ordinary of the Roman Curia
and of its districts, etc., etc.

To all and everyone who shall inspect these our present
letters, we certify and attest, that for the greater glory of the
omnipotent God and the veneration of his saints, we have
freely given to the Very Reverend Father Spratt, Master of
Sacred Theology of the Order of Calced Carmelites of the
convent of that Order at Dublin, in Ireland, the blessed body
of St Valentine, martyr, which we ourselves by the command
of the most Holy Father Pope Gregory XVI on the 27th day of
December 1835, have taken out of the cemetery of St
Hyppolytus in the Tiburtine Way, together with a small vessel
tinged with his blood and have deposited them in a wooden
case covered with painted paper, well closed, tied with a red
silk ribbon and sealed with our seals and we have so delivered
and consigned to him, and we have granted unto him power in
the Lord, to the end that he may retain to himself, give to
others, transmit beyond the city (Rome) and in any church,
oratory or chapel, to expose and place the said blessed holy
body for the public veneration of the faithful without, however, an Office and Mass, conformably to the decree of the
Sacred Congregation of Rites, promulgated on the 11th day of
August 1691.

In testimony whereof, these letters, testimonial subscribed
with our hand, and sealed with our seal, we have directed to be
expedited by the undersigned keeper of sacred relics.

Rome, from our Palace, the 29th day of the
month of January 1836.

RULE OF ST COLUMBA

The Church in Ireland stands as a shining light in the early Middle Ages. As a European monastic centre, it had no equals to match its missionary zeal, and faithful men such as St Columba and his followers went to Scotland to convert the heathen. Their influence stretched throughout northern Europe as many people left their pagan ways and embraced Christianity.

St Columba and his monks did not leave any written rules, preferring the guidance of Scripture to direct them. However, the following 'rule', attributed to St Columba, was practised much later and it shows the depth of the Irish faith:

- Be alone in a separate place near a chief city, if thy conscience is not prepared to be in common with the crowd.
- Be always naked in imitation of Christ and the Evangelists.
- Whatsoever little or much thou possess of anything, whether clothing, or food, or drink, let it be at the command of the senior and at his disposal, for it is not befitting a religious to have any distinction of property with his own free brother.
- Let a fast place, with one door, enclose thee.
- A few religious men to converse with thee of God and his Testament; to visit thee on days of solemnity; to strengthen thee in the Testaments of God, and the narratives of the Scriptures.
- A person too who would talk with thee in idle words, or of the world; or who murmurs at what he cannot remedy or prevent, but who would distress thee more should he be a tattler between friends and foes, thou shalt not admit him to thee, but at once give him thy benediction should he deserve it.
- Let thy servant be a discreet, religious, not tale-telling man, who is to attend continually on thee, with moderate labour of course, but always ready.
- Yield submission to every rule that is of devotion.
- A mind prepared for red martyrdom [that is death for the faith].

- A mind fortified and steadfast for white martyrdom [that is ascetic practices]. Forgiveness from the heart of every one.
- Constant prayers for those who trouble thee.
- Fervour in singing the office for the dead, as if every faithful dead was a particular friend of thine.
- Hymns for souls to be sung standing.
- Let thy vigils be constant from eve to eve, under the direction of another person.
- Three labours in the day, viz., prayers, work, and reading.
- The work to be divided into three parts, viz., thine own work, and the work of thy place, as regards its real wants; secondly, thy share of the brethen's [work]; lastly, to help the neighbours, viz., by instruction or writing, or sewing garments, or whatever labour they may be in want of, ut Dominus ait, 'Non apparebis ante Me vacuus [as the Lord says, 'You shall not appear before me empty'].
- Everything in its proper order; Nemo enim coronabitur nisi qui legitime certaverit. [For no one is crowned except he who has striven lawfully.]
- Follow alms-giving before all things.
- Take not of food till thou art hungry.
- Sleep not till thou feelest desire.
- Speak not except on business.
- Every increase which comes to thee in lawful meals, or in wearing apparel, give it for pity to the brethren that want it, or to the poor in like manner.
- The love of God with all thy heart and all thy strength.
- The love of thy neighbour as thyself.
- Abide in the Testament of God throughout all times.
- Thy measure of prayer shall be until thy tears come.
- Or thy measure of work of labour till thy tears come.
- Or thy measure of thy work of labour, or of thy genuflexions, until thy perspiration often comes, if thy tears are not free.

A. W. *Haddan and W. Stubbs*, Councils and Ecclesiastical Documents Relating to Great Britain and Ireland II, vol. i, *Oxford, Oxford University Press, 1873, pp. 119–21.*

THE FICTITIOUS SAINT

 It is thought that the legend of St Urho was created in 1956 by Richard Mattson, a retail store manager from Virginia in the USA as a rival to St Patrick. His joke story of the patron saint of Finland quickly gained credence and today St Urho's Day is celebrated in Finnish centres in Virginia, Minnesota and New York as well as cities in Finland.

Mattson's story was a simple retelling based on the legend of St Patrick, who is said to have expelled snakes from Ireland. In Mattson's version, St Urho was famous for driving out poisonous frogs from Finland! In some later versions, it is supposed to be grasshoppers rather than frogs.

It is thought that Mattson called the saint after Urho Kekkonen who became the President of Finland in March 1956. According to Mattson, Urho was a powerful man who gained his strength from fish soup (*kalla mojakka*)and sour whole milk (*feelia sour*).

There are varied rituals and ceremonies on St Urho's Day on 16 March that include Finnish national dishes, dressing up as grasshoppers, and wearing the saint's colours – purple and green. It is a day to party and celebrate all things Finnish. There is even an Ode to St Urho that is sometimes recited:

Ooksie, kooksie kollme vee
Santia Urho is the boy for me
He chase out the hopper as big as birds
Never before have I heard those words.

He really told those bugs of green.
Bravest Finn I ever seen.
Some celebrate for St Pat and his snake
But that Urho boy got what it takes.

He got tall and strong on *feelia sour*
And ate *kalla mojakka* every hour.
That's why that guy could chase those beetles
That crew as thick as jack pine needles.

So let's give a cheer
in our very best way
On the sixteenth of March
St Urho's Day!

(Incidentally, Finland's official national patron saint is Henry of Uppsala.)

THE CHIEF OF SINNERS

John Bunyan, the famous author of *The Pilgrim's Progress* and a spiritual giant, was born in Bedford in 1628. When he reached 16, he joined Cromwell's New Model Army and then became a tinker. Upon leaving military service, he joined the Puritan Free Church in Bedford and became a 'field preacher'.

This was a dangerous occupation in the reign of King Charles II and, in 1666, Bunyan was imprisoned in Bedford for his evangelical activities. While in prison, he wrote his spiritual autobiography – *Grace Abounding to the Chief of Sinners* – describing the spiritual change that occurred in his life from being a profane unbeliever to a fervent preacher and author. This extract from that book finds Bunyan typically expressing his lack of trust in himself (he referred to himself as 'a poor and contemptible servant of Jesus Christ') and his enduring need for God's grace:

I find to this day seven abominations in my heart: (1)

Inclinings to unbelief. (2) Suddenly to forget the love and mercy that Christ manifesteth. (3) A leaning to the works of the law. (4) Wanderings and coldness in prayer. (5) To forget to watch for that I pray for. (6) Apt to murmur because I have no more, and yet ready to abuse what I have. (7) I can do none of those things which God commands me, but my corruptions will thrust in themselves, 'When I would do good, evil is present with me.'

These things I continually see and feel, and am afflicted and oppressed with; yet the wisdom of God doth order them for my good. (1) They make me abhor myself. (2) They keep me from trusting my heart. (3) They convince me of the insufficiency of all inherent righteousness. (4) They show me the necessity of flying to Jesus. (5) They press me to pray unto God. (6) They show me the need I have to watch and be sober. (7) And provoke me to look to God, through Christ, to help me, and carry me through this world.

SEVEN DEADLY SINS, HEAVENLY VIRTUES, AND CORPORAL WORKS OF MERCY

Deadly Sins	Heavenly virtues	Corporal works of mercy
Pride	Faith	Feed the hungry
Envy	Hope	Give drink to the thirsty
Gluttony	Charity	Give shelter to strangers
Lust	Fortitude	Clothe the naked
Anger	Justice	Visit the sick
Greed	Temperance	Minister to prisoners
Sloth	Prudence	Bury the dead

TEN TWENTIETH-CENTURY MARTYRS

On 9 July 1998, the Archbishop of Canterbury, in the presence of Queen Elizabeth II, unveiled statues of ten twentieth-century martyrs outside the west front of Westminster Abbey. The ten martyrs commemorated were:

- Father Maximilian Kolbe (Zdunska Wola), a victim of Nazism in 1941. He offered his own life to save a fellow prisoner, Franciszek Gajowniczek, condemned to death by the camp authorities after a successful escape by a fellow prisoner.

- Manche Masemola, murdered by her parents for converting to Christianity in Transvaal (South Africa) in 1928.

- Janani Luwum, a school teacher from Uganda, murdered in 1976 by the Idi Amin regime.

- Grand Duchess Elizabeth of Russia, a victim of the Russian Revolution of 1918.

- Dr Martin Luther King Jnr, American preacher assassinated in Memphis in 1968.

- Archbishop Oscar Romero of San Salvador, murdered in 1980.

- Dietrich Bonhoeffer, German pastor murdered by the Nazis in April 1945.

- Esther John (Qamar Zia), Indian missionary, murdered in 1960.

- Lucian Tapiedi, from Papua New Guinea, murdered by Japanese troops in 1942.

- Wang Zhiming, Chinese pastor, executed by the authorities in 1973.

BIBLICAL TERMS FOR SIN

What is sin? The Bible uses many different terms to cover the basic tendency to do wrong that is inherent in every person. The Bible provides a comprehensive explanation for the existence of sin and how we can be set free from it now and for ever more. Here are some biblical terms for this much misunderstood and sorry state:

- The Old Testament has at least 8 Hebrew words to describe sin – *ra* meaning 'bad', *rasha* meaning 'wickedness', *asham* meaning 'guilt', *chata* meaning 'sin', *avon* meaning 'iniquity', *shagag* meaning 'err', *taah* meaning 'wander away', and *pasha* meaning 'rebel'. Perhaps the last term best describes the overall 'drive' of sin – it is rebellion against that which is right and true.

- The New Testament has at least 12 Greek terms to describe sin, including *kakos* meaning 'bad', *poneros* meaning 'evil', *absebes* meaning 'godless', *enochos* meaning 'guilt', *adikia* meaning 'unrighteousness', *agnoein* meaning 'ignorant', *anomos* meaning 'lawlessness', *parabtes* meaning 'transgression', *planan* meaning 'to go astray', *paratoma* meaning 'to fall away', and *hupocrites*, meaning 'hypocrite'.

The Bible does not make a distinction between serious (mortal) and not so serious (venial) sins, although the Catholic Church teaches this as one of its doctrines. The remedy of salvation by faith in Jesus, based upon the Grace of God, saves sinners from the penalty, punishment and presence of sin.

These truths are admirably expressed in Charles Wesley's popular hymn, 'Ye Ransomed Sinners Hear':

Ye ransomed sinners, hear,
The prisoners of the Lord;
And wait till Christ appear
According to His Word.

Rejoice in hope; rejoice with me.
Rejoice in hope; rejoice with me.

We shall from all our sins be free.
In God we put our trust:
If we our sins confess,
Faithful He is, and just,
From all unrighteousness
To cleanse us all, both you and me;
To cleanse us all, both you and me;

We shall from all our sins be free.
Surely in us the hope
Of glory shall appear;
Sinners, your heads lift up
And see redemption near.
Again I say: rejoice with me.
Again I say: rejoice with me.

ST BARTHOLOMEW'S DAY MASSACRE

On 24 August 1572 (St Bartholomew's Day), a great persecution began against French Protestants (Huguenots). The Huguenots (meaning 'sworn companions') were followers of John Calvin, who led a growing movement away from papal authority throughout France. These believers were encouraged in their endeavours by many French nobles and it seemed, for a time, that a substantial Protestant Church along the lines of Calvin's Geneva church could be established in France.

However, the growth of the Huguenots caused alarm at the Vatican and among the French court. Queen Catherine de' Medici demanded the death of the Huguenot leader, Admiral Coligny. This took place while the Queen's daughter,

Marguerite de Valois, was exchanging marriage vows with the Protestant Henry de Bourbon (King of Navarre – later King Henry IV). Indeed the wedding celebrations marked the start of a massacre that claimed the lives of thousands of Protestants, and Henry de Bourbon was the sole Huguenot survivor from the wedding party.

Anti-Huguenot violence spread from Paris throughout France leading to at least 30,000 deaths. This is part of an eye-witness account from the statesman and historian Jacques Auguste de Thou:

So it was determined to exterminate all the Protestants, and the plan was approved by the queen. They discussed for some time whether they should make an exception of the king of Navarre. All agreed that the king of Navarre should be spared by reason of the royal dignity and the new alliance. The Duke of Guise, who was put in full command of the enterprise, summoned by night several captains of the Catholic Swiss mercenaries from the five little cantons, and some commanders of French companies, and told them that it was the will of the king that, according to God's will, they should take vengeance on the band of rebels while they had the beasts in the toils.

After Coligny had said his prayers with Merlin the minister, he said, without any appearance of alarm, to those who were present: 'I see clearly that which they seek, and I am ready steadfastly to suffer that death which I have never feared and which for a long time past I have pictured to myself. I consider myself happy in feeling the approach of death and in being ready to die in God, by whose grace I hope for the life everlasting. For me it is enough that God is here, to whose goodness I commend my soul, which is so soon to issue from my body'.

Readings in European History, ed. J. H. Robinson, Boston: Ginn, 1906, pp. 179–83.

THE FORMULAE OF
ST EUCHERIUS

St Eucherius was the Bishop of Lyon in the fifth century. A noted scholar, he is known today for his 'formulas of spiritual intelligence' – a series of 'biblical proofs' in the style of logical statements. Eucherius believed, 'The divine scriptures first shine like silver but glow like gold in their hidden parts. Rightly it is so managed, because the purity of eloquence is hidden altogether from the promiscuous eyes of the crowd, as if it were covered by a garment of modesty. And so, the divine is taken care of by the best stewardship; the scriptures themselves protect the heavenly mysteries by cloaking them, just as divinity itself works in its own mysterious way.'

He wrote a series of formulae and this is an extract from the one entitled 'Names and Significance of the Members of the Lord':

The eyes of the Lord are understood by divine examination; Psalm 33: the eyes of the Lord are toward the righteous.

The ears of the Lord are worthy when they hear; Psalm 33: his ears are toward their cries.

The arms of the Lord are a help to his saints; Psalm 34: take up arms and a shield.

The protection of the Lord is a shield; Psalm 5: O Lord, you have crowned us with the shield of your goodwill.

The precepts of the Lord or of the Apostles are arrows; Psalm 17: he has sent his arrows and has scattered them.

The word of the Lord is living, and it is as efficacious and penetrating as a two-edged sword. (Hebrews. 4. 12)

The trumpet of God is the voice of the Lord made manifest; in the command and voice of the archangel and in the trumpet of God. (1 Thess. 4. 15)

The rod of the Lord is a sign of his rule or of the correction of discipline; Psalm 45: the rod of equity, the rod of your reign.

The staff of the Lord is the sustaining consolation of God; Psalm 23: your rod and your staff, they comfort me.

Fire is the Holy Spirit; Acts 2: and fire appeared to them in forked tongues and sat above each of them, and they were filled with the Holy Spirit.

THE LITTLE FLOWER OF JESUS

Marie-Françoise-Thérèse Martin, who is revered as St Teresa of Lisieux (France), is the latest Doctor of the Church. Born in 1873, this 'little flower of Jesus' only lived to the age of 23, but achieved much in her short life.

She entered the Carmelite order in Lisieux when she was just 15. The closeness of her walk with Jesus is attested to by her much loved writings. A childlike faith, a constant seeking after spiritual growth, knowledge of the Scriptures and her humility are the hallmarks of her 'little way'.

As an adolescent, Teresa yearned to be a saint and sought God to attain ever more holinesss – 'I desire to be a saint, but I know my weakness and so I ask you, my God, that you yourself be my holiness' – is one of her most famous sayings. She experienced a powerful conversion on Christmas Day 1886, after attending midnight Mass.

Unlike many other saints, there are no miracles recorded during Teresa's life, no special signs or great conflicts with secular authorities. Yet her ordinary existence attracts many pilgrims to Lisieux who come to celebrate her extraordinary relationship with God. Almost all we know of Teresa is through her writings (over 250 letters, 54 poems, 8 plays, over 20 prayers, and her 'Final Conversations') which began to be published a year after her death. Today, there are more than 50 editions of her works, and in 1993 her *Complete Works* were presented to Pope John Paul II.

This is an extract from a poem called 'My Hope', first published in 1896:

Though in a foreign land I dwell afar,
I taste in dreams the endless joys of heaven.
Fain would I fly beyond the farthest star,
And see the wonders to the ransomed given!
No more the sense of exile weighs on me,
When once I dream of that immortal day.
To my true fatherland, dear God! I see,
For the first time I soon shall fly away.

THE LEPER OF MOLOKAI

On 11 May 1873 the steamer *Kilauea* deposited 33-year-old Father Joseph Damien de Veuster on the landing at Molokai in the Hawaiian Islands. The Islands were ravaged with leprosy – the 'separating sickness' – which had come about as a result of the increased trading links in the seventeenth century. King Kamehameda V established a leprosarium on the island of Molokai, and in 1866 over 140 sufferers were banished to the island. Here the lepers were isolated and the rest of the population forgot about them.

However, the Catholic Church did not forget them and Bishop Maigret sent Father Joseph to minister to the lepers of Molokai. The plan was to send ministers on a rota basis to help the sufferers, but Father Joseph knew, after just a few days, that he would remain with them, and wrote back: 'I am bent on devoting my life to the lepers. It is absolutely necessary for a priest to live here. The afflicted are coming here by the boatloads.'

For the next 16 years, Father Damien served the growing leper community with Christ-like devotion. He cleaned wounds, bandaged ulcers, amputated gangrenous limbs, built shelters, laid pipelines for fresh water, dug graves and constructed some 1,600 coffins.

Because he lived with these afflicted people and embraced them, it was inevitable that Father Damien himself would contract leprosy. Nevertheless, he did not allow the thought of this to affect his work or faith. In 1888, he enlisted help to set up a girls' orphanage on the island, and three weeks before his ravaged body succumbed to leprosy he was still working hard to comfort his flock. A few days before he died in 1889, he said, 'The work of the lepers is in good hands and I am no longer necessary, so I shall go up yonder.'

On 4 June 1995, Father Joseph was beatified by Pope John Paul II, and today his memory is honoured by a statue that stands in the Rotunda of the US Capitol building. In 1969, when his case was considered for sainthood, Pope Paul VI said of Father Joseph Damien de Veuster: 'Love expresses itself in giving. Saints have not only given of themselves, but they have given of themselves in the service of God and their brethren. Father Damien is certainly in that category. He lived his life of love and dedication in the most heroic yet unassuming way. He lived for others: those whose needs were the greatest.'

THE CURÉ OF ARS

St John Vianney (1786–1859), the Patron of Parish Priests and the Curé of Ars in France, was a poor farmer's son who had much difficulty learning Latin and suffered many illnesses. Although he was ordained by the age of 30, he was considered incapable of leading a parish and needed further training. In short, Vianney had nothing to commend him.

He was very hard on himself but gentle with others. He lived on a diet of boiled potatoes, slept for just two or three hours, and kept himself suspended from the floor by a system of ropes to avoid rats.

However, St John had a remarkable healing ministry and

attracted many people to his services until his fame spread throughout France. A dedicated priest, he would often spend over 15 hours a day hearing confession. He conducted a great struggle against the taverns that encouraged drunkenness and eventually succeeded in banning alcohol in his parish. This is an extract from one of his sermons against the evils of drink:

St Paul in the Holy Bible assures us that the drunkard will not enter into the kingdom of heaven; drunkenness, therefore, must be a great sin. If drunkenness is a disease:

- It is the only disease contracted by an act of the will
- It is the only disease that requires a licence to propagate it
- It is the only disease that is bottled and sold
- It is the only disease that requires outlets to spread it
- It is the only disease that produces revenue for the government
- It is the only disease that is habit forming
- It is the only disease that produces crime
- It is the only disease that is permitted to be spread by advertising
- It is the only disease without a germ or virus and for which there is no corrective medicine
- It is the only disease that will condemn you to eternal separation from God in Hell. (Gal. 5. 21)

St John Vianney was canonized in 1925. It is said that his body has not decomposed.

THE FATE OF THE APOSTLES

Scripture does not record how the Apostles died, but tradition holds that they were all martyred or banished, as victims of Roman persecution:

Apostle	Cause of death
Peter	Crucified upside down in Rome – AD 66
Andrew	Crucified in AD 74
James, son of Zebedee	Beheaded in Jerusalem – AD 44
John, son of Alphaeus	Beaten to death in AD 60
John the Beloved	Banished to the Isle of Patmos – AD 96
Philip	Crucified in Phryga – AD 52
Bartholomew	Crucified in AD 52
Thomas	Run through by a lance in India – AD 52
Matthew	Slain with a sword in Ethiopia – AD 60
Simon	Crucified in Persia – AD 74
Mark	Died in Alexandria after being dragged through the streets
Thaddaeus	Shot by arrows – AD 72
Paul	Beheaded in Rome – AD 66

THE WIZARD OF BALWEARIE

Little is known for certain about Michael Scot(t), the legendary magician from the twelfth century who lived near Selkirk in Scotland. Tales of his prowess abound, but it is difficult to separate myth from historical fact. It is said that Scot possessed an unparalleled knowledge of magic, philosophy, astronomy, maths and physics. It is claimed he studied at Oxford, Paris, Padua, Bologna and Toledo universities.

He is said to have become a favourite of the Holy Roman

Emperor Frederick II by healing him of an incurable sickness. He was also supposed to own a magical horse that could transport him at fantastic speed from Scotland to Paris. On one occasion, Scot was so tormented by the demon that he commanded it to make rope from the sands of Kirkaldy beach, a task that is never ending!

The wizard's reputation seems largely based on Walter Scott's ballad, 'The Lay of the Last Minstrel', a mention in Dante's *Inferno* (among the magicians and soothsayers), and in a sixteenth-century Italian poem called 'Merlin Coccaius', an extract of which is given below:

> Behold renown'd Scotus take his stand
> Beneath a tree's deep shadow, and there draw
> His magic circle – in its orb describe
> Signs, cycles, characters of uncouth shapes;
> And with imperious voice his demons call.
> Four devils come – one from the golden west,
> Another from the east; another still
> Sails onwards from the south – and last of all
> Arrives the northern devil;
>
> 'Tis said that he who wears
> His magic cap, invisible may walk,
> And none so lynx-eyed as detect his presence,
> In the most peopled city – yet beware,
> Let him not, trusting to the demon's power,
> Cross the white splendour of the sun, for there,
> Although no palpable substance is discern'd,
> His shadow will betray him.

The Mirror of Literature, Amusement, and Instruction,
no. 492, vol. 17, Saturday, 4 June 1831

MAJOR MONASTIC ORDERS

Founder	Order	Habit
St Benedict	BENEDICTINE	Black
St Romualdo	Camaldolesi	White
St Bruno	Carthusians	White
St Bernard of Clairvaux	Cistercians	White
St Bernard dei Tolomei	Olivetani	White
St Philip Neri	Oratorians	Black
St John Gualberto	Vallombrosans	Light grey
St Augustine	AUGUSTINE	Black
St Bridget of Sweden	Brigittines	Black
St Norbert	Premonstratensians	Black or Brown
St Philip Benozzi	Servi	Black
St John de Matha	Trinitarians	White
St Peter Nolasco	Order of Mercy	White
St Albert of Vercelli	CARMELITE	Dark brown
St Theresa	Scalzi	Dark brown
St Dominic	DOMINICAN	White
St Francis of Assisi	FRANCISCAN	Brown or Grey
St Matteo di Bassi	Capuchins	Dark brown
St John of God	Cordeliers	Brown
St Francis de Paula	Minimes	Brown
St Bernardino of Siena	Observants	Grey

St Clara	Poor Clares	Grey or Brown
St Jerome	JERONYMITE	
St Ignatius Loyola	JESUIT	Black
St Francis de Sales	VISITATION OF MARY	Black

CURIOUS SAINTLY DEEDS
– PART FIVE

- St Vitus is the patron saint of dancers and actors and those who find it difficult to get up in the mornings! He was a Sicilian nobleman, who enraged his heathen father by converting to the Christian faith. As punishment he was beaten and cast into a dungeon. But he was attended by angels who danced in the prison in the midst of dazzling light. When the saint's father looked at the scene, he was blinded by the light, but St Vitus' prayers restored his sight. Today, he is noted for a neurological condition called St Vitus Dance (Sydenham's Chorea), characterized by involuntary limb movements and muscle weakness.

- St Zenobius was a fourth-century Bishop of Florence. He had a remarkable ministry of miracles and was much revered by the Florentines. He is said to have restored to life a man who died by falling from a church precipice. On another occasion, a mother bought her dead child to the saint and he prayed and brought the girl back to life. When St Zenobius died, such vast crowds gathered at his grave, to touch him one last time, that his body was pushed against a tree near the cathedral of Florence. The tree, though old and withered, at once produced fresh leaves!

- St Margret of Cortona lived a wild life in thirteenth-century

Tuscany. She had many lovers, but her life was transformed when one of them was murdered. A little dog guided Margaret to his body and she was so sticken by the sight that she tried to join the Franciscan convent at Cortona. However, they would not receive her because of her sinful past. But one day, when Margaret was praying, she saw Jesus motion towards her and she knew she was forgiven.

- St Charles Borromeo was the Archbishop of Milan in the sixteenth century. When the plague broke out in that city, many fled – but Charles remained to minister to the outcasts. Three times he walked barefoot through the city and, falling before the crucifix in the cathedral, offered himself as a sacrifice for the people. He was a great reformer and campaigned vigorously against religious abuses. Thus he made many enemies, and on one occasion a Franciscan friar fired a shot at him while Charles was at prayer. The bullet got caught in the material of his cape and he survived unharmed!

- St John Nepomuc of Bohemia was the confessor to the wife of Wenceslaus IV, Emperor of Germany in the fourteenth century. The Emperor wanted to know the confessions of his wife, but John refused to tell him. Enraged by his silence, the Emperor had John thrown into the River Moldau. As he sank, five stars in the form of a crown appeared over the spot. St John is the patron saint of silence, running water, bridges and also against slander.

THE PREACHER AND THE PIT

John Wesley, the founder of Methodism, was a famous preacher who covered thousands of miles on horseback to present the gospel throughout Britain. One of his strangest locations was Gwennap Pit, a large hollow formed by the collapse of old underground mines in St Day in Cornwall.

This was the ideal place for meetings because it was sheltered and Wesley's voice could be carried far and wide in the natural amphitheatre. Between 1762 and 1789, John Wesley preached 18 times at Gwennap Pit. The last occasion was when he was 86 and he recorded in his diary, 'I preached in the amphitheatre I suppose for the last time; for my voice cannot command the still increasing multitudes . . .'

Gwennap Pit became a popular open air 'pulpit' for many preachers after Wesley's death. Today, Methodists from around the world still gather at the Pit for the annual Whit Monday service and it has even been the location for a few wedding ceremonies!

SAINTS' AND SINNERS' QUOTES

The revealed truth of the Bible is not that Jesus Christ took on Himself our fleshly sins, but that He took on Himself the heredity of sin. God made His own Son 'to be sin' that He might make the sinner into a saint.

Oswald Chambers, My Utmost for His Highest

The only difference between the saint and the sinner is that every saint has a past, and every sinner has a future.

Oscar Wilde, A Woman of No Importance

Grace is indeed needed to turn a man into a saint; and he who doubts it does not know what a saint is.

Blaise Pascal, Pensées

Can one be a saint without God? This is the only problem I know of today.

Albert Camus, La Peste

Many of the insights of the saint stem from his experience as a sinner.

Eric Hoffer, The Passionate State of Mind

Many people genuinely do not wish to be saints, and it is probable that some who achieve or aspire to sainthood have never felt much temptation to be human beings.

George Orwell, Shooting an Elephant

I fear that Christians who stand with only one leg upon earth also stand with only one leg in heaven.

Dietrich Bonhoeffer, letter to his fiancée, 1943

Christians have burnt each other, quite persuaded
That all the Apostles would have done as they did

Lord Byron, Don Juan

Christ beats his drum, but he does not press men; Christ is served with voluntaries.

John Donne, Sermons, no. 39

He that will not live as a saint, can never die a martyr.

Thomas Fuller, Gnomologia

Men die only for that by which they live.

Saint-Exupéry, Flight to Arras

The International Thesaurus of Quotations,
ed. Rhoda Thomas Tripp, Penguin, 1970

SAINTS AND THEIR FLOWERS

For centuries, the *sanctorale*, the calendar of saints, provided a useful way of marking the natural passing of the seasons and the agricultural year. Many saints were remembered by association with what the land produced at the time of their martyrdom. This is an early English church calendar giving the flowers linked to saints and their feast days:

While the Crocus hastens to the shrine
Of Primrose love on St Valentine
Then comes the daffodil, besides
Our Ladyes-Smock at our Ladye-tide.
About St George, when blue is worn,
The blue Harebells the fields adorn;
Against the daie of Holie Cross,
The Crowfoot gilds the flowerie grasse.
When Barnabie bright smiles night and daie,
Poor Ragged Robin blossoms in the haie.
The Scarlet Lynchnis, the garden pride,
Flames at St John the Baptist's tide.
From Visitation to St Swithin's showers,
Lilie White reigns Queen of the floures.
And Poppies, a sanguine mantle spred,
For the blood of the dragon St Margaret shed.
Then under the wanton Rose, again
That blushes for Penitent Magdalen.
Till Lammas daie, called August's Wheel,
When the long corn stinks of Cammamile,
When Mary left us here belowe,
The Virgin's Bower is fullin blaw;
And yet anon, the full Sunfloure blew,
And became a starre, for Bartholomew.
The Passion-Floure long has blowed,
To betoken us signs of the Holy Roode . . .
The Michaelmas Daisies, among dede weeds,
Blooms for St Michael's valorous deeds.

And seems the last of floures that stroude,
Till the feste of St Simon and St Jude.
Save Mushrooms and the Fungus race,
That grow till All-Hallow-tide take place.
Soon the ever-green Laurel alone is greene,
When Catherine crowns all learned menne.
The Ivie and Holly berries are seen,
And Yule-log and wassails come round agen.

Flora Sancta, *Norwich, Canterbury Press*

CURIOUS SAINTLY DEEDS
– PART SIX

• St William of Bourges, who died in 1207, always wore a hair-shirt and never ate meat. When he was dying, he asked for his body to be laid on ashes in his hair-shirt. His relics were venerated for over 300 years and supposed to work many miracles. It is said that a bone of his arm is still at Chaalis in France, and one of his ribs at Paris.

• St Ulrick, who died in 1154, was born near Bristol. He became a priest, and kept dogs and hawks for sport, till he met a beggar who asked for alms. When Ulrick said he didn't know if he had anything to give, the beggar said, 'Look in thy purse, and you shall find twopence halfpenny.' He found as he was told and gave it to the beggar, who prophesied that Ulrick would become a saint. He was a hermit, fasting often, at Hessleborough in Dorset. He never slept unless he could not stay awake, and slept leaning against a wall. Waking up, he would chastise his body for being so lazy. After a hair-shirt became too comfortable, he changed it for an iron coat of mail. In winter he sat in a tub of cold water reciting psalms.

- St Vincent was a Spanish martyr said to have been tormented by fire, so that he died in 304. His body was thrown in a marshy field among rushes, but a crow defended it from wild beasts and birds of prey. Tradition records that the crow drove away birds and fowls greater than himself, and that it chased a wolf with his beak.

- Jesuit accounts record that Emperor Alexander IV wanted St Martina as his wife. She refused him, so the Emperor commanded her to be tortured. The Jesuits' stories of these operations and her escapes are wonderfully particular. According to them, hooks and stakes did her no mischief; she had a faculty of shining, which the pouring of hot oil upon her would not quench; when in gaol, men in dazzling white surrounded her; she could not feel 118 wounds; a fierce lion, who had fasted three days, would not eat her, and fire would not burn her; but a sword cut her head off in 228, and at the end of two days two eagles were found watching her body.

- St Mildred was the first Abbess of Minster, in the Isle of Thanet, founded by King Egbert in about 670. The Minster was built by command of the King to expiate his murder of his two nephews, Etheldred and Ethelbright. Mildred's relics were taken St Augustine's monastery at Canterbury in 1033. They were venerated above all the relics there, and worked many miracles. The churches of St Mildred, Bread Street, and St Mildred in the Poultry, London, are dedicated to her.

CURIOUS DEEDS OF
ENGLISH SAINTS

- St Elphege (or Alphege) became Bishop of Winchester in 1006 and Archbishop of Canterbury. He was imprisoned in Greenwich by the Danes who overran Kent and London in 1011. While in prison the devil appeared to him in likeness of an angel, and tempted him to follow him into a dark valley, over which he wearily walked through hedges and ditches. At last the devil vanished, and a real angel appeared and told St Alphege to be a martyr. He was slain by the Danes in 1012 and is buried in St Paul's in London.

- St John of Beverley was Bishop of Hexham, a village in the North of England. Several miracles are related to him, including his ability to calm fierce bulls and healing oil issuing from his sepulchre in 1312. He is also supposed to have inspired King Ethelstan to victory over the Scots.

- St Aldhelm founded the Abbey of Malmesbury, and was the first Englishman to cultivate both Latin and English. He lived a life of strict discipline and used to recite the psalter at night, plunged up to the shoulders in a pond of water. His biographers say that while in Rome he turned a sunbeam into a clothes-peg to hang his vestments! He died in 709.

- Bede's *Ecclesiastical History* records St Alban as being the first martyr (in 303) in Britain. Alban was from Verulamium (now the town of St Albans) in Hertfordshire. He is supposed to have converted his executioner, caused a river to dry up, and a fountain to appear on the summit of the hill where he was executed.

- St Walburg (or Walburga) was born in 710, in Devonshire, the daughter of King Richard, sister of St Willibald and St Winebald. In 748, she left England to evangelize Germany as part of St Boniface's mission. She had amazing skills of healing and is the patron saint of those afflicted by plague, rabies and coughs.

- St Chad was born in 673 and became the founder and bishop of the see of Lichfield. He is famous for blessing a local well that offered miraculous cures, causing thousands of people to crowd to the site. According to Bede, before the saint died, there was 'joyful melody as of persons sweetly singing descended from heaven for half an hour, and then mounted again to heaven'.